ID0803530

Eighteenth Century
English Poetry

Eighteenth Century English Poetry

Peter Thorpe

Nelson-Hall Co.

nh

Chicago

Library of Congress Cataloging in Publication Data
Thorpe, Peter.
   Eighteenth century English poetry.

   Bibliography: p.
   Includes index.
      1.   English poetry—18th century—History and
criticism.   I.   Title.
PR551.T45 1975   821'.009   74-17807
ISBN 0-88229-196-3

ISBN 0-88229-196-3

Copyright© 1975 by Peter Thorpe

All rights reserved. No part of this book may be reproduced
in any form without permission in writing from the publisher,
except by a reviewer who wishes to quote brief passages in
connection with a review written for broadcast or for inclusion
in a magazine or newspaper. For information address Nelson-Hall
Company, Publishers, 325 W. Jackson Blvd., Chicago, Illinois 60606

Manufactured in the United States of America

821.09
T3981e

To:
Peggy Scout

149906

Table of Contents

Preface

This book is designed for the student rather than the teacher, critic, or scholar. Its purpose is to make the bewildering variety of genres and traditions of eighteenth-century English poetry accessible in a simplified form. It does not seek to provide a definitive statement about Augustan verse, but rather a place to start. With the exception of satire, the complexity of which calls for special treatment, I have tried to keep the discussions brief.

In treating a genre or tradition, I have had four objectives in mind: to give a definition; to furnish some history; to discuss the ways in which the tradition manifests itself in the period; and to suggest some reasons for its popularity—or unpopularity—in the period.

At the end of the book is a bibliography (grouped by chapter) of modern and eighteenth-century works that I have found useful. The bibliography makes no claim to be exhaustive; in a few cases, I have omitted some "major" works because I have found them dull or intimidating.

This book, then, is a doorway to eighteenth-century poetry, and beyond that, it offers some guideposts for further study. It is a reference work, and need not—and should not—be read straight through. Though it marshals a good many facts, it tries to avoid getting bogged down in them; therefore, such pendants as constant references to dates and critics are kept to a minimum. On the other hand, because the assessing of genres and traditions is at best a subjective business, I have not refrained from theorizing and criticizing in the course of my discussions. The reader will notice, for example, that I attempt to work out some unorthodox ideas about the georgic-pastoral relationship, about the topographical poem, and about the familiar and heroic epistles.

Anyone who writes about genres is confronted with an ontological problem: What is the mode of existence or essence of a tradition or a "kind," especially after it has lain abandoned by writers for two centuries? I believe it is best to describe a type of literature not in terms of *what is does*, but in terms of *what it does that is striking*.

A mundane but useful analogy to this approach is our impression of a certain small foreign car. If asked to describe this car, we would say that it is shaped like a beetle. But we would also mention its distinctive and unmistakable sound, a kind of asthmatic gargle. Yet how many hours per day does this automobile make such a noise? The average owner probably drives no more than an hour in twenty-four hours at best. Most of the time, then, the "beetle" does *not* do what we say it does, even though we know we are justly representing it in our description.

The same case holds true for traditions of literature. We remember the heroic couplet chiefly because of its architecture, balance, antithesis, parallelism, and well-placed caesuras—even though not every couplet will have these characteristics. But it is the architecture of the heroic couplet that makes it memorable, and it is this salient feature that I have centered on in my discussion of the couplet tradition. Dealing with what is striking is, by and large, my approach to all of the genres and traditions covered in the following chapters.

The flexible terms "eighteenth century" and "Augustan" make frequent appearances in this volume. The eighteenth century is at least 140 years long (1660–1800), and at times it is even longer (if one recalls the appearance of Denham's *Cooper's Hill* in 1642 or Crabbe's *The Borough* in 1810). "Augustan" is even more flexible, for scholars have used it to mean anything from the reign of Queen Anne (1702–1714) to the period 1660–1800. In this book the terms are allowed to keep their flexibility, with the expectation that the context will make clear what is meant each time they are used.

The numerous quotations from poets are, whenever possible, taken from the reliable standard editions; but spelling and punctuation in most cases have been modernized. Regarding the paying of scholarly debts, it should be assumed that this work is indebted to everything mentioned in its bibliographies. Where the debt involves the direct use of a specific source, I have made this clear in the bibliography.

A word about the level of difficulty. Faced with a possible choice between insulting the reader's intelligence and talking over his head, I would incline toward the latter. I hope that constant reference to a number of minor writers, as well as to the major ones, will not put the student off but instead will show him the busy-ness and the wealth of the genres and traditions.

Finally, I would reaffirm one of the book's basic assumptions—that the discussion in genres is more analytical and interpretative than descriptive, and that the reader should realize that ultimately he must identify Augustan poetry in his own terms. In the meantime, the following pages offer a place to begin.

I

The Town

In this chapter the genres or kinds covered are: the familiar epistle, epigram, epitaph, fable, mock-heroic, burlesque, some minor mock genres, formal verse satire, and the prologue-epilogue. What all of these have in common is not only their emphasis on man as a social creature, but also their strong inclination toward satire. Such a variety of witty genres suggests that satire is best looked upon as a spirit or temper of writing that can inhabit any number of genres or traditions of prose or poetry. (For a theoretical discussion of satire, see Chapter V.)

Familiar Epistle

The familiar epistle is a verse letter, almost always written in heroic couplets, usually addressed to an intimate of the poet, and customarily delivered in a casual or relaxed style. It may be of any length, but ordinarily it consists of a hundred to four hundred lines. Its subject matter ranges from the highly serious (e.g., Pope's study of the master passion in his

Epistle to Cobham) to the low and ludicrous (e.g., Goldsmith's *Haunch of Venison: A Poetical Epistle to Lord Clare*). It may, and frequently does, include extended satire (e.g., Pope's *Epistle to Arbuthnot*).

The familiar epistle takes for its classical model the *Satires* and *Epistles* of Horace; and, like Horace, the Augustan tries to achieve an effect of apparent casualness of structure or arrangement with a definite coherence under the surface. Horace was long admired for this trick of studied casualness: Oldham's imitation of *Ars Poetica* praises "the easy and familiar way of writing, which is peculiar to Horace in his Epistles"; Dryden claims that he wrote his dedication of the *Aeneid* after the excellent manner of Horace, "in a loose epistolary way"; Shaftesbury's *Characteristics* lauds Horace's *Epistles* and *Satires* for their "concealment of order and method" and their "extemporary air"; and *Spectator* 618 declares that a poet writing according to the example of Horace's epistles must arrange his work so that "everything he says [will] be in a free and disengaged manner."

The familiar epistle has two audiences—the poet's intimate, who is the specific addressee, and the public at large. This gives the writer the advantage of seeming to speak very sincerely and personally while addressing the public. One has the impression from reading the epistle that it is a pregnant discourse, highly intimate and revealing, that the reader is privileged to overhear. To create this impression, the author can use either dialogue or monologue. There is occasionally an attempt by the poet to create a kind of dramatic situation between himself and the addressee, but in almost every case the main emphasis is on what the author has to say rather than on the recipient's response to it. Thus the addressee often emerges as a kind of plastic or flexible sounding board similar to some of the colorless auditors of Socrates.

The structure of the familiar epistle, as already observed, strives for seeming casualness. Beyond this it can be remarked that a great number of these pieces exhibit a structure that tends to fall into two parts: casual beginning and orderly end. Addison's *Letter from Italy*, for example, begins its address to Lord Halifax with a general and somewhat rambling description of Italy. Then, about two-thirds of the way through, the poet begins to zero in on his main thesis, about which there has been little hint heretofore, that Britain's liberty is superior to Italy's tyranny, even though Britain's land and climate are much more harsh than those of Italy.

Another example that shows this eddying type of beginning and focused ending is Swift's *Horace, Epistle VII, Book I, Imitated and Addressed to the Earl of Oxford*. In this poem the thesis that Oxford has tended to destroy Swift rather than help him does not emerge until roughly halfway through the work's 138 lines. Similarly, Pope's *Epistle to Cobham* gives the reader only a slight hint of what is coming: The first two-thirds deal, in a digressive way, with the inscrutability of human character; only in the final third does one discover the main point, which is that to find the master passion is to find the key to the whole man. All three of Burns's *Epistles to Lapraik* exhibit the structure described above. In the second one, for instance, Burns begins with a wandering casualness during which he touches on his preparations for writing; in the second half of the poem, one discovers that the main point is the upholding of rural simplicity over the decadence of sloth and wealth in the city.

Churchill's *Epistle to William Hogarth* at first glance seems to go against Horace's "graceful negligence" (an expression found in Oldham, Dryden, and Pope); for all the way through it is a steadily focused, intense attack. Yet a closer look reveals that the first part (lines 1–212) is really a dissertation on satire that could be prefixed to any number of Augustan poems. Even the attack on Hogarth does not make its actual thesis clear until fairly near the end; only at a very late point in the poem does the reader learn that the real issue is that Hogarth has *misused* his great talents. In the meantime one has had to wade through, among other things, a vicious series of insults aimed at Hogarth's physical features.

The structure of the familiar epistle, then, tends to divide itself into two sections: disorder and order. This is the pattern of numerous epistles throughout the Augustan Age—not *simultaneous* order and disorder, but casualness *followed by* order. When the epistles are produced in groups, as in the *Epistles to Lapraik* or in John Byrom's four *Familiar Epistles to a Friend,* the structure starts over with each new letter.

Just what this structure means (if one assumes structure itself contains meaning) is not clear. However, two theories present themselves. One is that the structure means that the familiar epistle, in that it tends to bring order out of disorder, is essentially comic (not necessarily laughable) and optimistic. Another theory is that the Augustan, a lover of order, needs a kind of temporary chaos with which to illuminate by contrast his ideal—what better way to do this than through the familiar epistle, which almost always offers such a contrast?

The familiar epistle may be said to begin its history, as far as English literature is concerned, with the close of the medieval period in the works of such writers as Erasmus and Sir Thomas Wyatt. However, the first major flourishing of the genre does not occur until the Elizabethan golden age—that is, the closing decades of the sixteenth and the opening few years of the seventeenth centuries. It is in this period that one finds such highly successful works as Thomas Lodge's *A Fig for Momus* (containing seven verse epistles), Donne's *Letters to Several Personages,* and Jonson's famous letter *Inviting a Friend to Supper* (which the poet calls an "epigram"). From this point until the close of the eighteenth century, the verse letter was to remain an extremely popular form. If one had to locate a high point in the production of such missives, it would not be inaccurate to say that the verse epistle seems to be most active in the fourth decade of the eighteenth century; but in any case, it enjoyed a vogue lasting two hundred years.

Reasons for such popularity are not hard to find. The main one, of course, was the enormous prestige of Horace, an ancient who not only gave laws but also furnished ocular proof of his creative ability. Another reason, only slightly less important, was that the doctrine of restraint put the Augustan poet in the position of having to speak not as private lyricist but as public gentleman. The familiar epistle, then, was a way for the poet to maintain his public image while allowing him to say a few private things at the same time, as has been pointed out in the earlier remarks about the double audience. Again, the familiar epistle gained popularity through having been exploited by some of the very best writers. Dryden wrote excellent epistles to Congreve the playwright and to Kneller the painter; and later in the period, Pope's brilliant epistles were probably the main cause of the rise of epistolary production to such a height in the 1730s. Familiar epistles are so much a main part of eighteenth-century poetry that no student can afford to skip lightly over them.

Epigram and Epitaph

An epigram is customarily thought of as a short, concise poem concluding with a flash of wit. It takes all subjects for its province, but its most common topics are love and the characters of people. In English it is usually in heroic couplets but may appear in any meter. The original meaning of the word epigram is "inscription," and the ancient Greeks at first used it in this sense. It is interesting to surmise that the inherent brevity of the genre may owe something to the difficulties of chiseling letters into a restricted space on a marble block.

As has often been pointed out, the structure of the epigram falls into two parts. First, the poet directly or indirectly presents the reader with something that arouses his curiosity or instills in him a feeling of anticipation. Then, in the last line, or in the last words or *word* of the last line, the poet delivers, usually in the form of wit, the solution or answer to the problem raised in the earlier part of the poem.

In many epigrams the curiosity-arousing object

or problem is presented not in the poem itself but in the title or in the knowledge that the reader already has of the subject. Thus it is not surprising to note that the titles of some epigrams are longer than the poems to which they are attached. Nor is it unusual to find that the reader must furnish some background knowledge. Pope's brilliant epitaph on Sir Isaac Newton—"Nature and nature's laws lay hid in night; / God said, *Let Newton be!* and all was light"— would not be clear to the uninformed tourist who had no idea of the great mathematician's accomplishments or influence. The structure of the epigram, then, falls into two parts; but at least some of the time, the first part lies outside of the poem itself.

Concerning the mood or tone of the epigram, one can see two central traditions. For the sake of convenience, the earlier one can be designated the *Greek Anthology* tradition, taking its name from the famous large collection of short poems composed by several hundred authors over some seventeen centuries, starting in the seventh century, B.C. (The *Greek Anthology* is sometimes called the *Palatine Anthology* because it was discovered—in the seventeenth century—in the Palatine Library at Heidelberg.) For the most part, the epigrams by the earlier writers in the *Greek Anthology* lack the irony and bitterness, the sharp points of wit and satire that one usually associates with this genre; but they are epigrams nonetheless.

Poets in this tradition of epigram writing are more interested in a kind of pleasant gracefulness; they try to produce "a set of fine thoughts, but of such a kind as neither create mirth or surprise; they are only capable of giving pleasure to very delicate tastes, by a natural and elegant expression." This description, quite adequate for the *Greek Anthology* tradition, appeared in the preface to *A Collection of Epigrams* published in London in 1727 (the writer was probably William Oldys). The critic went on to say that "good sense, and pure language, somewhat raised above ordinary conversation, are all that are necessary to constitute a Greek epigram." Though the criticisms are adequate, the term "surprise" is used in a rather special sense; for any epigram worthy of the name will work, if it is successful, at least a little sudden wonderment upon the reader.

The second epigram tradition, already implied in the above paragraphs, may be designated the Martialian, after the Latin poet Martial, who was active in the first century, A.D. In the poetry of Martial one immediately sees the pointed wit, the irony, the satire, and frequently the bitterness that modern readers normally associate with the epigram. Martial characteristically ends with a sharp turn of thought or "point," whereas the *Greek Anthology* epigram more often ends with a pregnant or sententious statement, gentle and not biting.

The above, then, are the two central traditions of the epigram. To avoid an oversimplification, however, it should be mentioned that not all of Martial's work is caustic or satiric; some of his best pieces deal tenderly with such matters as the death of a beautiful child. On the other hand, a great number of the epigrams by the later writers in the *Greek Anthology* are very much in the typical Martialian manner—sharply witty, satiric, and somewhat jaundiced in their view of mankind. But it is safe to use *"Greek Anthology"* and "Martialian" as tags with which to separate two different tendencies in the genre.

The history of the epigram in English begins, as does the history of many a genre, in the Renaissance. The early humanists (Sir Thomas More especially) wrote good epigrams; and by the turn of the sixteenth-seventeenth centuries, both the *Greek Anthology* and Martialian traditions were firmly established. One would be hard put to say which tradition was winning out at this time, for some of the best poets, notably Jonson and Herrick, practiced both with equal facility. On the other hand, Sir John Harington, the most accomplished epigrammatist of the Renaissance, chose the Martialian tradition and produced hundreds of caustic pieces.

Harington was with the tide of the future, for the Augustan Age was to be essentially Martialian in its handling of the epigram. It is difficult to find an eighteenth-century poet who did not write epigrams, and it is almost as difficult to find an Augustan writing consistently in the *Greek Anthology* tradition. The Martialian epigram remains a very strong trend in literature from 1660 to 1800 and beyond. That the *Greek Anthology* epigram tends to disappear in this period may be due to Augustan skepticism about the lyric; but even when, at the close of the eighteenth century, the lyric begins to reemerge, there is very little slackening in the production of Martialian epigrams.

What made the epigram appeal to the Augustans is a matter of speculation. But it can be ventured that the pithy, summary conciseness of the genre well suited the eighteenth-century people's temperament; for they set a value on order and certainty and positiveness (this is not to say they achieved these virtues). They liked the epigram because it seemed to imply that things could be closely defined and pinpointed. They also liked the genre because, from the time of the later writers of the *Greek Anthology*, it had lent itself to the battle of satire, and satire was always palatable to the Augustan. And their love of the heroic couplet, which as early as the Renaissance had become the standard meter for the epigram, made the genre congenial to their view of things.

The above is not to imply, however, that the Martialian epigram keeps the same identity from the sixteenth through the eighteenth centuries. For one thing, the Elizabethans frequently employed wordplay or puns to ignite the flash of wit at the end of the poem. The Augustan, on the other hand, had a tendency to look down upon such verbal shenanigans, as is clear from the dissertation attributed to Oldys: the epigram should not employ "jingle of words, pun, quibble, conundrum, mixed wit or false wit" ("false wit" is used here in the sense that Addison had used it in *Spectator* 35). But not all eighteenth-century writers obeyed such dictums. Shenstone plays on the word *Kidderminster*, a coarse woolen cloth, in his epigram entitled *On Mr. C__ of Kidderminster's Poetry*: "Thy verses, friend, are Kidderminster stuff, / And I must own you've measured out enough."

The Augustan also differed from the Elizabethans in that he tried to clean up the epigram, which since the time of Martial had had about it a kind of prurient, bawdyhouse atmosphere. But that the eighteenth century was not always successful in this effort may be seen in such pieces as Matthew

Prior's hilarious (to the broad-minded) epigram *On a Fart, Let in the House of Commons.*

A third difference between the Renaissance and the Augustan epigram occurs in the matter of length. Some of Ben Jonson's approach one hundred lines, and not a few of Harrington's are in the twenty-to-thirty-line range. The eighteenth century preferred a shorter epigram, averaging perhaps six lines or less. But Oldys (?) was liberal enough to acknowledge that an epigram can be of any length, as long as the writer uses no "more words than are necessary to introduce and express the conceit he drives at." Marital himself wrote an epigram attacking a person who said that his epigrams were too long; and one of Martial's epigrams runs to forty-two lines. There was classical precedent, then, for long epigrams, but the love of summary pithiness in the eighteenth century seemed to call for a shorter poem.

No one knows how many epigrams were produced in the Augustan Age, but they ran easily into the tens of thousands. It is possible that Pierre Nicole's claim to have perused approximately fifty thousand epigrams in preparation for his *Epigrammatum delectus* (1659) is not exaggerated. That Nicole rejected a huge majority of these shows the scarcity of good epigrams. They are scarce in eighteenth-century England, too, but no one is sorry that such poets as Pope wrote such items as the epitaph on Sir Isaac Newton. There is enough of this sort of quality in the period to warrant the student's attention.

There is little difference between epigram and epitaph. Both genres aim at brevity; both frequently employ heroic couplets; both allow either serious grace of thought or pointed wit (i.e., *Greek Anthology* and Martialian). Beyond that, one can go into the backwaters of literary history and point out that there was an argument about whether Latin or English should be used—a famous incident in Boswell's *Life of Johnson* is Johnson's refusal to "disgrace the walls of Westminster Abbey with an English inscription" (said in connection with preparations for Goldsmith's interment). While Johnson has the floor, it may be appropriate to remark that he allowed a certain amount of kindly omission in epitaphs of villains *(An Essay on Epitaphs)*, and that in his *Life of Pope (Lives of the Poets)* he quipped that the fact that Pope had to borrow from himself in writing epitaphs showed "the scantiness of human praises."

Elsewhere in the backwaters of literary history, one learns that in the eighteenth century there was a sort of fashion of writing epitaphs for oneself; such pieces were composed by Gay, Prior, and many others. Gay's is pointed and famous: "Life is a jest; and all things show it / I thought so once; but now I know it." Prior's is touching and serious: "To me 'twas given to die: to thee 'tis given / To live: alas! one moment sets us even./ Mark! how impartial is the will of Heaven!"

Fable

A fable is a short tale designed to illustrate a moral. Because the characters in the story are usually animals behaving as humans or as human *traits*, the fable can be said to partake of allegory.

There is a kind of built-in contrast between the animal and the human, and human nature often shows up as inferior to animal nature. For example, the fox who said the grapes were sour is exhibiting a reaction found only in the realm of man; in the back of his mind the reader knows the fox itself is innocent.

The fable usually ends with a proverb or maxim; it has been accurately said that many fables are in reality proverbs acted out or dramatized. The action is brief, the characters are few, and the tale is short— ordinarily somewhere between twenty and sixty lines in the poetic fable. In England the iambic tetrameter couplet is the favorite meter for the genre, but poets have tried a number of different forms.

The history of the fable probably begins almost as far back as the history of mankind, for it seems to be a central human impulse to illustrate morality with exempla, as can be seen in any number of mythologies, including the Bible and classical mythology. To give a full history of the fable is, if one is not restrictive, to give a history of literature. For the sake of brevity, several high points in the development of the genre can be singled out.

Though much anticipated by earlier literature, the first main event in the fable tradition is the famous collection attributed to Aesop, the Greek slave who flourished around 600 B.C. The next major happening occurs in the Orient, in the *Panchatantra* (meaning "five headings" in Sanskrit), a group of tales that seems to have been gathered sometime between 300 and 500 A.D. These tales use animals as characters and are generally of high quality and of a very humorous nature. By the Middle Ages they had made their way into Europe and thus, together with Aesop, had some influence upon the medieval "beast epic," the most famous example of which is Chaucer's *Nun's Priest's Tale* dealing with the rooster Chauntecleer.

By the neoclassical period, then, three major influences had been established: classical, oriental, and medieval English. Perhaps it would have been surprising if the Augustan had not turned his attention to the fable. The three great neoclassical or eighteenth-century collections of fables are those produced by Jean de La Fontaine, the late-seventeenth-century French writer (very influential in England); those written by John Gay, the Augustan poet; and those assembled by Gotthold Lessing, the late-eighteenth-century German dramatist and critic. It is not startling to find an Augustan in this honored list, for the eighteenth century in England achieved immortality at least once in every genre it set its hand to.

Gay was not the only one in his era to write or render a successful poetic fable. Other poets who did well in this vein were, to name only a few of them, Dryden, Swift, Byrom, Prior, Smart, Cowper, and Beattie. Even Johnson participated, producing his short but brilliant *The Ant*, based on Proverbs 6:6. But Gay's work was by far the best in the period, and thus any discussion of the Augustan fable would do well to begin with this "favorite of the wits."

In his *Life of Gay (Lives of the Poets)*, Johnson gave the following definition:

A fable or apologue . . . seems to be, in its genuine state, a narrative in which beings irrational, and sometimes inanimate, *arbores lo-quuntur, non tantum ferae,* are, for the purpose of moral instruction, feigned to act and speak with human interests and passions.

But Johnson felt that Gay sometimes strayed from this definition:

To this description the compositions of Gay do not always conform. For a fable he gives now and then a tale or an abstracted allegory; and from some, by whatever name they may be called, it will be difficult to extract any moral principle. They are, however, told with liveliness; the versification is smooth, and the diction, though now and then a little constrained by the measure or the rhyme, is generally happy.

With due respect to Johnson, one might speculate that one of the reasons for the enormous success of Gay's fables is that Gay *did* violate the genre. It is possible that had the poet plodded through the same pat formula over and over again, without sometimes deviating into "tale" or "abstracted allegory," his fables would be little read today. Their success owes a great deal to the Augustan tendency to enrich and vary a genre, never taking it at face value, never becoming enslaved to it. In fairness to Johnson, it can be said that he acknowledged that several definitions of the fable were possible; however, he did seem to feel that one should commit oneself to a particular definition. This is, fortunately, what Gay refused to do.

If one were to pick up an early edition of Gay's first series of *Fables,* he would be struck by a wood-

cut frontispiece depicting a dramatic mask whose expression suggests neither misery nor joy but rather
something in between. Such an indefinable expression is a kind of key to the tone of the first series of
Fables; for although the poems abound in humor,
their underlying theses seem frequently to show a
kind of *Weltschmerz* or disillusioned cynicism toward mankind. As in much modern drama, comic
means are used to achieve tragic ends. Typical of this
pattern is Fable XIV, "The Monkey Who Had Seen
the World." The earlier part develops images of the
monkey "made captive in a lady's room" and such
light and silly items as references to the monkeys as
"hairy sylvans." But the ending is somber in its application of the story to "the dull lad," who
"O'erlooks with scorn all virtuous arts."

In a general sense it can be said that all of Gay's
Fables, and a great many fables written by other
writers of many different eras, have but one major
theme. This is *man's foolish pride*. A good example is
Matthew Prior's *A Fable from Phaedrus* (a second-
rate Roman imitator of Aesop); it is unusually short
and can be quoted in full:

> The fox an actor's vizard [mask] found,
> And peered, and felt, and turned it round:
> Then threw it in contempt away,
> And thus old Phaedrus heard him say:
> "What nobler part canst thou sustain,
> Thou specious head without a brain?"

There is the old persistent thesis: the foolish
vanity of mankind—his ceaseless aspirations to be
something more than what he really is.

Christopher Smart, who like Gay loosens the genre to include not only animals but people, inanimate objects, and allegorical passions and ideas, wrote a number of fables. They are generally of a lighter atmosphere than those of Gay, but nonetheless deal with the same ultimate problem—man's vanity in seeking to be something other than himself. As good an example as any is *The Tea Pot and Scrubbing Brush,* in which the brush satirizes the vain teapot for putting on airs.

Incidentally, all of the fables referred to so far use the customary meter of iambic tetrameter couplets. In order to keep the discussion brief, only two more examples will be touched on; both are by Swift, who made some interesting variations in the genre. *A Fable of the Widow and her Cat* is significant because, unlike most of the Augustan fables, it does not use the four-stress couplet. *The Fable of Midas* is noteworthy because it shows the connection between classical myth and the fable, and because it also shows the fable being used to attack a political opponent. Indeed, there is scarcely such a thing as an eighteenth-century genre that cannot be used for attack.

Not everyone in the eighteenth century was charmed by the fable. Joseph Warton, while not wholly against the fable tradition, seemed to feel that very little first-rate work had been done in the genre in England. Digressing on Gay in his *Essay on the Genius and Writings of Pope,* Warton declared that Gay's fables, the most "popular of all his works, have the fault of many modern fable-writers, the ascribing to the different animals and objects introduced, speeches and actions inconsistent with their several natures." But this raises the question of where the animals get "their several natures" in the first place—from the imagination of man, of course. Warton's narrow view would exclude a large part of the entire tradition of the fable and restrict the fable writer to a mechanical scheme that would soon have died of its own repetition.

A more serious charge against the fable was leveled by Thomas Chatterton in his poem *Fables for the Court*. The boy-poet implies that the chief difficulty with fables, and with numerous other literary genres, is that at present they are obscure or lack meaning:

> What has the author to be vain in,
> Who knows his fable wants explaining,
> And substitutes a second scene
> To publish what the first should mean?

But Chatterton is no doubt overstating the case somewhat, for the Augustan fable is usually simple and to the point; when it isn't, the moral attached at the end will clear things up.

Before going on to inquire into the reasons for the popularity of the fable in the Augustan period, a minor problem in vocabulary needs to be solved. "Fable" in the eighteenth century could have two meanings: one is the sense in which this discussion has been using the word; the other meaning is "plot," and a number of eighteenth-century critics—Addison and Johnson, for example—use it in this sense as well as in the first sense. It should be stressed that to talk about plot is not necessarily to talk about the fable; for in the typical fable, the story line is sketchy and not at all important. Indeed, the fable as practiced in the eighteenth century almost misses completely the category of narrative. Therefore, it would be more accurate to call the fable an image or a succession of images.

There are probably a great many special reasons why the Augustans found the fable so compatible. Some strong possibilities are the period's love of didacticism, love of traditional or classical literature, and love of the theme of man's foolish pride, for which the fable seemed to be an excellent vehicle. Probably the strongest of these three reasons is didacticism; for from Dryden's *Preface to the Fables* to Johnson's *Life of Gay*, the rule that the fable should provide "moral instruction" is heavily stressed. But the Augustan liked his instruction sweetened *(dulce et utile)*, and he found the cleverly-written fable to be among the tastiest of sugar-coated pills. Sometimes the sugar was especially pungent, as in Gay's *The Wild Boar and the Ram* (Fable V, First Series), in which the peaceful Ram calmly points out that his hide furnishes parchment for unethical legal wrangling and coverings for the drums of war—"The two chief plagues that waste mankind."

Mock-Heroic, Burlesque, and Some Minor Mock-Genres

Put in the simplest terms, mock-heroic is that species of writing using high style and low subject matter; its opposite, which is called "burlesque" in this discussion, uses low style and high subject matter. Because in the Augustan Age the mock-heroic was more popular than the burlesque, it seems appropriate to begin with the former.

Mock-heroic may be subdivided into two main sections: mock-heroic and mock-epic. Mock-heroic occurs when the poet's aim is not so much to tell a story (epic involves narrative) as to cause laughter merely by exploiting incongruities between style and subject. The most successful mock-heroic of the Augustan Age is John Philips's *The Splendid Shilling*, which deals with a fearful debtor in a pseudo-Miltonic style—pompous Latinisms, inverted syntax, heroic similes, and circumlocutions:

> Afflictions great! yet greater still remain:
> My galligaskins that have long withstood
> The winter's fury and encroaching frosts,
> By time subdued, (what will not time subdue!)
> An horrid chasm disclose, with orifice
> Wide, discontinuous; at which the winds
> Eurus and Auster, and the dreadful force
> Of Boreas, that congeals with Cronian waves,
> Tumultuous enter with dire chilling blasts
> Portending agues. Thus a well-fraught ship
> Long sailed secure, or through the Aegean
>   deep,
> Or the Ionian, till cruising near
> The Lilybean shore, with hideous crush
> On Scylla or Charybdis, dangerous rocks,
> She strikes rebounding, whence the
>   shattered oak,
> So fierce a shock unable to withstand,
> Admits the sea....

The speaker is talking about a hole in his trousers.
As distinct from the mock-heroic, the mock-epic

furnishes a *narrative*, accompanied by the customary devices of epic as practiced by Homer, Virgil, or Milton: invocation; division into "books" or "cantos"; heroic battles and games; windy descriptions of warriors' armaments (deriving ultimately from Homer's description of Achilles' shield); interference by the gods; descents into the underworld; long pompous speeches; and, as in mock-heroic, epic or heroic similes. Like the mock-heroic, mock-epic exploits incongruities between subject and style; but unlike mock-heroic, it concentrates on some trivial narrative made all the more trivial by the massive epic machinery that moves it along—or encumbers it.

As far as the Augustans are concerned, the first main event in this tradition is Dryden's *Mac Flecknoe* (1682); but the most brilliant piece of mock-epic work is generally acknowledged to be Pope's *Rape of the Lock*, a generation later. Pope's story, based on an actual incident, is that of a lord who has stolen a lock of a lady's hair; the theft brings about great "heroic" feats of battle and other ponderous classical machinations. The opening is like a great bugle blast:

What dire offence from amorous causes springs,
What mighty contests rise from trivial things,
I sing—This verse to Caryll, Muse! is due:
This, even Belinda may vouchsafe to view:
Slight is the subject, but not so the praise,
If she inspire, and he approve my lays.
Say what strange motive, Goddess! could
    compel
A well-bred lord to assault a gentle belle?

Caryll, a friend of Pope, suggested the topic in the hope that it might patch up the quarrel arising from the "rape." Though Pope was not successful in this objective, he did manage to furnish posterity with a magnificent piece of mock-epic writing.

Although Pope and Philips produced the most memorable of their types, mock-heroics or mock-epics proliferated in the period, especially in the early 1700s. Some of the better ones are: Dr. Samuel Garth's *Dispensary* (attacking apothecaries or druggists); Gay's *Fan* (dealing with the "origin" of the fan and possibly influencing Pope); Richard Blackmore's *The Kit-Cats* (Blackmore had been unsuccessful in the serious epic); Anne Finch's *The Battle between the Rats and the Weasel* ("In dire contest the rats and weasel met"); Pope's *Dunciad* (in many versions; somewhat vitiated by its extreme topicality); Allen Ramsay's *The Battle, or Morning Interview* (invasion of a lady's boudoir); Giles Jacob's *The Rape of the Smock* (the reader may compare Pope and draw his own conclusions); William Somerville's *The Bowling-Green* (echoing Waller's serious *On St. James Park*?); William King's *The Toast* (pretends to be a Latin poem rendered into English); William Hawkins' *The Thimble* (parts of it imitate Gay and Pope); and Peter Pindar's (John Wolcot) *Lousiad* (an "unfortunate" louse is "condemned to die"). But there was never again anything like *The Rape of the Lock*.

Mock style is not stable or consistent. It can be seen that in such works as *The Splendid Shilling* the style is not always high or "heroic." Perhaps the reader noticed in the passage quoted earlier the word *galligaskins*, which, though it derives from French, Italian, and Greek, was by Philips's time a perfectly common English word; thus at this point, the style has descended from the heroic to the ordinary. Indeed, it is hard to find a mock-heroic or mock-epic poem that does not at some point descend to ordinary language; the opening of *The Splendid Shilling* names well-known London public houses and such humble items as "oysters" and "ale."

The matter becomes complicated when one tries to analyze Philips's use of the epic simile. To the predicament of the constantly hunted debtor, the poet applies this analogy:

> So, poets sing,
> Grimalkin, to domestic vermin sworn
> And everlasting foe, with watchful eye
> Lies nightly brooding o'er a chinky gap,
> Protending her fell claws, to thoughtless mice
> Sure ruin.

One is hard put to classify this passage either as high or as low style, for some sort of fusion seems to have occurred. On the one hand, the very concept of attaching such a bulky simile to the poem is heroic; on the other hand, the *subject matter* of the simile, Grimalkin the housecat hunting mice, is low and humble and therefore nonheroic. One is forced to say that the style of the passage is neither high nor low but a fusion of both.

More often, however, the mock-heroic or mock-epic poem is a process of the style simply moving up and down. In Canto IV of *The Rape of the Lock,* for instance, one can observe a gradual stylistic descent. First, the gnome looses a bag of furies at the unfortunate Belinda—a heroic happening. Then there is a speech by Thalestris, the language of which is close to polite conversation of the day: "Methinks already I your tears survey, / Already hear the horrid things they say." And finally the poet strikes the bottom in the slangy jargon of Sir Plume: "My Lord, why, what the devil? / Z——ds! damn the lock! 'fore Gad, you must be civil!" Thus in the mock-epic there can be a number of styles at work.

The various styles of *The Rape of the Lock* can be seen in the narrator's voice, too. The two main ones are narrator-as-serious-epic-storyteller and narrator-as-buffoon. The first needs no illustration, for it occupies the bulk of the poem. But occasionally the narrator takes a recess from his strenuous epic duties to play the fool. When this happens, the style immediately plummets to the ludicrous: "Here living teapots stand, one arm held out, / One bent; the handle this, and that the spout." The reader of mock-heroic or mock-epic, then, can increase his enjoyment if he will remain on the lookout for a number of levels of style within the poem. Incidentally, such stylistic oscillations are not an innovation of the eighteenth century, for they occur occasionally in Homer and Virgil.

When one turns from the mock-heroic or mock-epic to the burlesque (high subject matter and low style), he is once again presented with a variety of styles within the poem. The most famous example of the burlesque is the early Restoration piece *Hudibras*, by Samuel Butler. It was to have enormous influence, and there are any number of "Hudibrastic" pieces in the eighteenth century, especially in the first half.

Hudibras, the story of a foolish puritan knight, is

rendered in rollicking tetrameter couplets that frequently use comic rhymes: "And pulpit, drum ecclesiastic, / Was beat with fist instead of a stick." The idea is to try to keep the style generally less dignified than the subject. But what actually happens is that, as in poems in the mock-heroic tradition, the style moves up and down, and the problem is complicated further by the hero having at once dignity (knighthood) and no dignity (the fact that knighthood, after the manner of Cervantes, is made to look foolish).

Even though the burlesque tradition fathered by *Hudibras* produced a number of works, it was never as popular or successful as the mock-heroic and mock-epic. It would be difficult to name one true Hudibrastic poem outside of Butler's work that is read today by anyone other than specialists, whereas the twentieth-century reader is usually familiar with at least a few mock-heroic or mock-epic poems other than *The Rape of the Lock*.

The Augustans did not, of course, invent the mock-heroic. For example, there was the *Battle of the Frogs and Mice*, long attributed to Homer; Chaucer's *Nun's Priest's Tale*, dealing heroically with the exploits of Chauntecleer the rooster and his seraglio; and in the Renaissance, Spenser's *Muipotmos* or "The Fate of the Butterfly." The Augustan would have been familiar with all of these and perhaps, too, with much of the mock-heroic traditions that were so strong in sixteenth-century Italy and in seventeenth-century France. Nor did the Augustans invent the burlesque, though fewer earlier examples of this genre exist. The Greek rhetorician Lucian composed the *Dialogues of the Gods*, in which those great

149906

immortals are made to look quite undignified; and Chaucer was to figure again as he burlesqued the great knight in his *Tale of Sir Thopas.* But though the Augustans were thus anticipated, they can be said to have brought burlesque, mock-heroic, and mock-epic to perfection.

It seems appropriate while on the subject of mock-literature of the eighteenth century to mention a few minor trends. One can begin with the generalization that practically every genre at one time or another came in for its share of mockery. The ode, for example, became a vehicle for irreverent humor in Gray's famous *Ode on the Death of a Favorite Cat, Drowned in a Tub of Goldfishes.* The normally serious elegy was exploited in numerous elegies on deaths of animals and in Swift's bitter *Satirical Elegy on the Death of a Late Famous General.* The georgic was snickered at in Gay's *Trivia,* and there were any number of mock-eclogues. The familiar and heroic epistles, too, were used mockingly. There were humorous epitaphs, and John Wilmot, Earl of Rochester, even went so far as to compose a flippant piece entitled *The Mock Song.* Scarcely a genre escaped the great deluge of mockery.

Purists have often said that, in writing such mock-poetry as the above, the poet was mocking something outside the genre, never the form or tradition itself. It has been held, for example, that Pope could respect the epic (in his translation of Homer) and still produce the magnificent *Rape of the Lock.* However, it would seem that the mere fact of choosing a once-serious genre for comic purposes implies at least a modicum of disrespect.

Formal Verse Satire

When a writer produces a satirical poem of several hundred lines with which he speaks rather directly *as* a satirist, most critics are inclined to call it "formal verse satire." If the poet speaks through an elaborate narrative or fiction, as in *The Rape of the Lock,* most critics are inclined to call it something else. Definitions of formal verse satire are vague at best, but a tentative formulation might be as follows: A formal verse satire is a poem of several hundred lines, usually in five-stress couplets, in which the supposed vices and follies of society are attacked in a general manner by a persona or speaker who willingly identifies himself as a satirist.

Like most satires, formal verse satire often has a random and casual structure. When it is more organized, it usually falls into two main sections: part "A," in which the targets are attacked; and part "B," in which the poet offers his solutions to the problems he pointed out in part "A." The first part, the survey of evils, is almost always much longer than the norms or positive ideals offered at the end. The truth seems to be that evil is simply more interesting to write about. And it is a truism among satirists of the eighteenth century that one must know evil in order to do away with it. In his *Essay Upon Satire,* Walter Harte wrote, "O Decency, forgive these friendly rhymes, / For raking in the dung-hill of their crimes." And a few years later (1737) Thomas Creech said in his preface to his translation of Horace that "Satire is to instruct, and that supposes a knowledge and discovery of the crime." If the central image of formal verse satire is often the foul muck of evil, we need not be surprised.

The origins of formal verse satire are obscure, but it seems to have existed at least as early as Archilochus, an ancient Greek writer who is traditionally looked upon as the inventor of the iambic meter, which originally was used for satire only. Going back further than Archilochus, one could argue that some of the Old Testament prophets, particularly Isaiah and Micah, also read like formal verse satirists. It may be that formal verse satire was born the moment man first possessed poetry *and* satire.

The two great ages of formal verse satire are ancient times in Rome and the late sixteenth century in England. In Rome the two major figures are Horace and Juvenal (both very popular in Augustan England) with Persius placing a distant third. Also worth mentioning is Lucilius, referred to by Horace and Juvenal in their satires and considered to be the father of Roman satire. Major figures in the English Renaissance are Hall, Marston, and Donne, the last named being by far the best.

In the eighteenth century, the best formal verse satirists are the Horatian Pope and the Juvenalian Johnson. In the second rank are John Oldham, Edward Young, Charles Churchill, and George Crabbe. Though there was a significant amount of formal verse satire produced by Augustan writers, this period achieved most of its satirical triumphs in other ways—such as travel literature *(Gulliver)*, mock-heroic *(The Rape of the Lock)*, or parody *(Shamela)*.

We return to our original premise that the great ages of formal verse satire are classical times in Rome and the Renaissance in England. On the other hand, anyone who has read Pope's brilliant *Imitations* of Horace or Johnson's magnificent *Vanity of Human Wishes* (imitating Juvenal's Tenth Satire) must surely realize that formal verse satire in the Augustan Age is well worth knowing about.

Prologue-Epilogue

Virtually every play produced in the Restoration and eighteenth century was preceded by a prologue and followed by an epilogue. Sometimes, like a train with extra engines and cabooses, a play would have two prologues and two epilogues. These pieces were in the neighborhood of twenty-five to fifty lines, with the epilogue, for obvious reasons of audience fatigue, tending to be a bit shorter. The meter was almost always heroic couplets. The couplets of the prologue-epilogue seem rather loose, open, and uncompressed when compared to those of a poem designed to be read rather than recited. The poet who wrote for the stage had to be sure that his message would get through upon first hearing. The slack pace and openness of the stage couplet can be seen in Pope's *Epilogue to Jane Shore:*

> Well, if our author in the wife offends,
> He has a husband that will make amends.
> He draws him gentle, tender, and forgiving,
> And sure such kind good creatures may be
>   living.

This passage, written within a year of *The Rape of the Lock,* is vastly different from the almost hectic, pithy, epigrammatical compression of the mock-heroic poem. As a popular poet, Pope certainly could have written all of the prologues and epilogues he wished to write. The fact that he wrote only a few makes one wonder if he felt uncomfortable in the almost too relaxed syntax of the stage couplet.

Though prologues and epilogues were designed to be recited on the stage, it was not uncommon for them to be printed for reading *after* they had been used in the theater. They often appeared in such periodicals as *The Gentleman's Magazine* and were sometimes collected in anthologies, such as *The Essence of Theatrical Wit: Being A Select Collection of the Best and Most Admired Prologues and Epilogues, That Have Been Delivered from the Stage* (1768), or the enormous four-volume *A Collection and Selection of English Prologues and Epilogues, Commencing with Shakespeare and Concluding with Garrick* (1779). Such anthologies were especially popular in the last half of the 1700s. The way in which these poems could so easily be detached and printed by themselves underscores a truism about the prologue-epilogue: They seldom had anything to do with the accompanying drama. Nor was it unusual to attach serious prologues to comedies, comic epilogues to tragedies, or other combinations. Very often the prologue-epilogue was written by someone other than the playwright; occasionally it would be someone who had neither read nor attended the play.

A good way to get further acquainted with this genre is to ask a basic question of it: What is its purpose? One of the prologue's functions was to warm up the audience, to work the spectators into a receptive mood that would ensure the success of the play.

The amazing thing is that in a few cases second- or even third-rate dramas were saved by brilliant prologues. An example is Richard Cumberland's lame *The Choleric Man,* which was rescued by the dazzling stage poetry of David Garrick the famous actor, who was also acknowledged by many to be the finest writer of prologues in the 1700s (the best in the Restoration was Dryden).

If the prologue could warm up the audience, the epilogue could cool them off and hopefully prevent some of the hissing and booing that might naturally emanate from hearty Augustan playgoers, no matter how good the play. A constant refrain in epilogues from 1660 to 1800 is a plea for the audience to applaud the play and respect the playwright. There is classical precedent for this, of course, for Plautus, the Roman writer of New Comedy, often makes a similar plea at the end of his plays. And in ancient Greek comedies such a plea might come right in the middle, as in Aristophanes' *The Clouds,* a drama in the Old Comedy tradition.

Throughout the Augustan period the writers of prologues and epilogues relied heavily on their wit. In the Restoration the satire was often directed *against* the audience (as in Dryden's bitter *Prologue to Aureng-Zebe*); whereas after 1700 the level of hostility was considerably reduced, so that author, actor, and playgoer frequently laughed together. The wit of the prologue-epilogue was often obscene, though as manners reformed after the Restoration, the obscenity was tempered if not actually suppressed. It has been said that the scurrility was for the underlings or rabble in the cheap seats or standing-places; in truth, most eighteenth-century folk, from lords and ladies to lackies and laborers, enjoyed a good dirty joke.

Though the prologue-epilogue is correctly identified as a wit-packed kind of poem, it is important to note that it could also convey serious moral lessons, as if complying with the major Augustan doctrine of *dulce et utile* (art should instruct as well as please). In his *Prologue ... in Drury Lane,* one of the finest of all prologues, Johnson argued the necessity for the public to insist on high moral standards in the drama:

> The drama's laws, the drama's patrons give,
> For we that live to please, must please to live.
>   Then prompt no more the follies you decry,
> As tyrants doom their tools of guilt to die;
> 'Tis yours this night to bid the reign commence
> Of rescued nature and reviving sense;
> To chase the charms of sound, the pomp
>   of show,
> For useful mirth and salutary woe;
> Bid scenic virtue form the rising age,
> And truth diffuse her radiance from the stage.

Any student of the history of drama knows that Johnson's plea went unheeded; the age continued to produce, with a few exceptions, thoroughly undistinguished plays. But it did go on to produce a great many excellent prologues and epilogues.

That *both* the playwright and the audience have a stake in the theater is a strong theme in the prologues and epilogues from Dryden to Byron. Such a close relationship between those on both sides of the footlights (not invented until well into the

Augustan period) was possible in the smallish theaters of the age. There was much less intimacy in the larger theaters of the nineteenth century, and such an atmosphere was inimical to the cozy friendliness of the prologue-epilogue. Also contributing to the death of the genre in the Romantic era was the ever-increasing popularity of musicals and burlesques, plays that normally did not use the prologue-epilogue. It has been suggested that Romanticism itself helped to do away with the prologue-epilogue, but it could just as well be argued that the chatty informality of this type of poetry could have served the causes of Romanticism. Perhaps the genre had simply worn itself out. As early as 1704 Nicholas Rowe (in his *Epilogue to The Biter*) was complaining about the burden:

> Of all the taxes which the poet pays,
> Those funds of verse, none are so hard to raise
> As prologues and as epilogues to plays.

And in 1732 Fielding referred to the prologue as "useless" though "necessary" *(Prologue to The Old Debauchees).*

As mentioned earlier, two main functions of the prologue-epilogue were to soften and to instruct the audience. To these may be added a number of lesser functions: to voice principles of taste and literary criticism; to acknowledge the presence in the theater of royalty or other dignitaries; to celebrate the opening of a new theater; to attack enemies of the playwright; to comment on politics; to satirize fashion; to enhance the career of a particular actor or actress (Pope's *Epilogue to Jane Shore*, referred to earlier, was expressly written for Anne Oldfield); and to make predictions about the future of English drama. Among these predictions might have been the demise of the prologue-epilogue at the close of the Augustan Age.

II

The Country

The genres or traditions discussed here are: pastoral, georgic, topographical poem, reflective-descriptive tradition, and the "graveyard school" of poetry. Also treated in this chapter is poetic diction, the elaborate verse language so dear to the Augustans and so odious to the Romantics. Poetic diction plays an important part in the kinds discussed in this chapter but is by no means restricted to them.

Pastoral

For the Augustans, a pastoral was a poem that had as its main function the creation of an image of rural innocence or happiness. It was felt to be literature of smooth verse and light subject matter, and frequently it contained the traditional pastoral elements associated with the classical models (Theocritus, Virgil, Bion, and Moschus): laments of love-struck shepherds; singing or piping contests for carved wooden drinking bowls or fancy flutes; and

elegies for dead shepherds. But more often the eighteenth-century pastoral extended itself into other
areas of subject matter, so that one finds such pieces
as: "town eclogues" (*The Basset Table*, ascribed to
Pope; Lady Mary Wortley Montagu's *Monday: Rox-
ana, or the Drawing Room;* or Andrew Erskine's *The
Street Walkers;* plus some of Swift's scatological
poems); occasional fishing pastorals (Moses Browne's
Piscatory Eclogues); political pastorals (Soame
Jenyns's *The Squire and the Parson: An Eclogue*);
foreign or "oriental" pastorals (Collins's *Persian Eclogues*); sea pastorals (John Draper's *Sea Eclogues*);
and the sacred pastoral (Pope's *Messiah*). Nor does
this list exhaust the possibilities. (Incidentally, the
term "eclogue," which originally meant merely a
"selection" and later meant a pastoral containing a
dialogue, is too broad a term to be of much use in discussions of pastoral.)

What can easily be deduced from the variety of
the above examples is that the Augustans, supposedly slaves to the doctrine of restraint, were ac-
tively resisting this restraint by expanding the
possibilities of the genre. Indeed, the trend had been
underway in the Renaissance with such works as the
Piscatory Eclogues of Giles Fletcher (1633) and
earlier, in the late sixteenth century, with the "extra-
pastoral" content of parts of Spenser's *Shepherd's
Calendar*. But the impetus to overflow the strict
pastoral limits was there in Virgil, whose *Eclogues*
contain political meanings. Or, at the risk of pedantry, one could point out that Virgil was merely carry-
ing on in the manner of Theocritus, who at the outset
of the pastoral tradition had allowed into the genre
such foreigners as reapers and fishermen. In short,

the pastoral had always lent itself to variety and expansion, and this is especially true in the eighteenth century.

As the examples given earlier might indicate, one method of resisting the confines of the genre was the use of humor, as in (to name the more successful) Pope, Lady Montagu, and Swift. In *The Basset Table*, a character with the facetious name of "Smilinda" makes it clear that the reed-pipe or the carved drinking bowl has been replaced by the snuff-box:

> This snuff-box—once the pledge of
>   Sharper's love,
> When rival beauties for the present strove;
> At Corticelli's he the raffle won;
> Then first his passion was in public shown;
> Hazardia blushed, and turned her head aside,
> A rival's envy (all in vain) to hide.
> This snuff-box,—on the hinge see brilliants
>   shine:
> This snuff-box will I stake; the prize is mine.

Sometimes, however, pastoral humor took a curious (and unintentional) turn, so that *The Shepherd's Week*, in which John Gay hoped to satirize the silliness of such writings as Ambrose Philips's *Pastorals*, turned out to be a very good, thoroughly English pastoral in its own right. In "Friday; or the Dirge," Grubbinol recalls the rural activities of the late Blouzelinda with highly visual and sharply realistic touches:

> Sometimes, like wax, she rolls the butter round,
> Or with the wooden lilly prints the pound.

This is probably as close as eighteenth-century pastoral ever got to sniffing the fresh, invigorating air of the English countryside.

That the pastoral might apply itself to just about anything is further illustrated by another humorous work of Gay, *The Beggar's Opera,* which Swift classified as a "Newgate pastoral." As long as the pastoral kept its humor and its ironic detachment, it could be successful poetry; when it took itself too seriously, it was frequently in danger of presenting the reader with the grossest of fatuities, of which Ambrose Philips's *Pastorals* are a very strong example. Here, from the *Sixth Pastoral,* is an unintentionally ludicrous induction to the inevitable singing match:

> Begin then, boys, and vary well your song;
> Nor fear, from Geron's upright sentence,
>   wrong.
> A boxen haut-boy, loud, and sweet of sound,
> All varnished, and with brazen ringlets bound
> I to the victor give: no small reward,
> If with our usual country pipes compared.

It is a rare thing to find in eighteenth-century literature a thoroughgoing, serious pastoral that can appropriately be called first-rate poetry.

Thus it was no wonder that even during the period the pastoral frequently found itself under attack. Although Johnson saw possibilities for a true English pastoral, much of his prejudice against the genre emerges in his famous denunciation of Milton's *Lycidas*:

Its form is that of a pastoral, easy, vulgar, and therefore disgusting: whatever images it can supply, are long ago exhausted; and its inherent improbability always forces dissatisfaction on the mind. *(Lives of the Poets: Milton)*

Johnson could just as accurately have applied the same anathema to many eighteenth-century pieces. And Pope, who had written the best traditional pastorals of the century, later admitted that they were trifles in which "pure description held the place of sense" *(Epistle to Dr. Arbuthnot)*. Much later in the century, the traditional pastoral was still under attack, as is evidenced by numerous passages in Crabbe's *Village*:

Yes, thus the muses sing of happy swains,
Because the muses never knew their pains.

At approximately the same time, Cowper was sneering at "self-deluded nymphs and swains" in Book III of *The Task*. A summary statement might be that the genre was very close to being worn out even at the beginning of the century and that this continued to be the case until the close of the period.

Although the history of the pastoral in the Augustan period is complex, it can be suggested in a short statement. Around the turn of the seventeenth-eighteenth centuries there were two main schools of pastoral thought. One can be designated the Theocritus-Fontenelle-Philips school (after the ancient poet, the neoclassical French critic, and Ambrose Philips), which tried to use a fairly realistic rural sub-

ject matter and to paint the pastoral world "as it is."
The other line of thinking may be termed the Virgil-
Rapin-Pope school (after the ancient poet, another
neoclassical French critic, and Alexander Pope),
which wished to show the pastoral scene not "as it
is" but as it "ought to be." As Pope expressed it,
pastoral should strive to give the reader "a perfect
image of that happy time" of the "Golden Age," the
period before the world fell into decay (Discourse on
Pastoral Poetry). But it should not be assumed that
the Theocritus-Fontenelle-Philips tradition was bru-
tally realistic; it was realistic only in relation to the
opposing school. Very little eighteenth-century
pastoral is "realistic" in the sense that a twentieth-
century audience would give to the term, and the
modern reader will usually find himself snickering
at the naiveté and inanity of the Augustan pastoral.

As the century moves into its second half, one
finds the Virgil-Rapin-Pope school all but deceased,
and the pseudo-realism of the Theocritus-Fontenelle-
Philips school on the rise. The trend continues until
the end of the century and culminates in Wordsworth (e.g., Michael). But lest one give the great Romantic too much credit, it should be noted that the
georgic tradition had long since taken a realistic look
at rural life and that, on the other hand, the Lake Dis-
trict and Wordsworth's image of it are frequently
two different matters.

Modern criticism is understandably hostile
toward Augustan pastoral; it is not as a rule front-
rank poetry, and the eighteenth century had already
set a precedent by damning itself on this point. But it
would be unfair to dismiss peremptorily all of the
pastorals of the period, for there are two important

defenses of the genre that ought not to be over-looked. One is simply that the eighteenth-century poet *intended* his pastorals for light reading; the other defense, paradoxically, is that the Augustan pastoral is quite capable of containing, under its polite surface, serious and complex meanings.

Since the discovery that pastoral "puts the com-plex into the simple," critics have noticed that a great part of this literature has a habit of using the rural matter as a means for the expression of the complex and sophisticated thoughts of the writer and his audience, who, after all, were highly edu-cated and not really interested in rustics *qua* rustics. This simple-as-complex point can be demonstrated in what is perhaps the best pastoral of the century, Pope's *Summer*.

Pope's world view involved images of order, stability, and harmony. To Pope, and to many who agreed with him, these ideas *were* the complex ex-perience of sophisticated men—exactly the sort of experience that a poet like Pope (probably un-consciously) might objectify in the simple matter of a pastoral poem. It is not difficult to find the above world view just under the surface in *Summer*. The love-struck shepherd begins his lament:

Ye shady beeches, and ye cooling streams,
Defense from Phoebus', not from Cupid's
    beams,
To you I mourn, nor to the deaf I sing,
The woods shall answer, and their echo ring.
The hills and rocks attend my doleful lay,
Why art thou prouder and more hard
    than they?

The kind of harmonious universe posited in the *Essay on Man* is suggested here both in subject matter and style. In subject matter, one can observe three mainsprings of Pope's cosmos: plenitude, continuity, and gradation. If, as Pope declares in the *Essay on Man*, "all must full or not coherent be," then the microcosm in these lines is coherent indeed, for Pope has drawn a complete circle and filled it with water, land, trees, sky, "hills," and "rocks"; even the woods are filled with life, for they "answer" and they have an "echo." Almost everything is in the plural; the little universe is one of plenitude and continuity. Gradation, the idea that a universe of plenitude and continuity must of necessity be informed by a "vast chain of being" or hierarchy, is suggested in some of the adjectives: "shady," "cooling" (not "cool"). The trees and water are put there for the purpose of serving man who, at least in Pope's golden-age universe, is above them in the scheme of things.

Having established this harmonious microcosm, Pope can then argue that the disdainful lover is out of harmony—the woods "answer" and "the hills and rocks attend," but she is willfully and wrongfully "deaf." In short, she is prideful. And in Pope's time, one way to show pride was to disrupt the harmony of things by stepping out of place in the Great Chain of Being.

The sense of order and harmony appears in Pope's pastoral style too, not just in the musical flow of the couplets but also in their architectonics. A parsing of the rigorously regular syntax of these lines appears in the discussion of the heroic couplet (p. 151).

Augustan pastoral, then, while seldom coming

up to the level of major poetry, can be well worth reading—not always, but often enough.

Georgic

To the eighteenth century, a georgic was a poem that purported to teach its readers, in a pleasurable manner, some kind of activity or process usually associated with rural life. Other common themes in the georgic are: dissertations on the art of weather forecasting; discussions of seasons; descriptions of nature; occasional brief narratives; and fictitious or mythological accounts of the origins of things, as in Gay's humorous story of the origin of the patten, a shoe for wet weather (*Trivia; or the Art of Walking the Streets of London*, Book I). The georgic is unapologetically didactic, regardless of its subject matter. It may appear in any poetic form but usually chooses couplets or blank verse for its medium.

Scholars have found English georgics as early as the fifteenth century, but until the eighteenth century there is no such thing as a poem closely modeled on the *Georgics* of Virgil. Thus such a piece as Thomas Tusser's long poem *Husbandry* (1557) emerges as a kind of literary accident, for it seems to owe little to Virgil. The Augustan georgic, shaped and influenced by the tradition of Virgil and, to a lesser degree, the *Works and Days* of Hesiod, begins with John Philips's *Cyder* (1706) and Gay's *Rural Sports* (1720). The next main events in the tradition are Somerville's *The Chase* and Tickell's *Fragment of a Poem on Hunting* (both 1735). From this point until the close of the century, the georgic gains strength to the point at which it would take a fairly large catalogue to name all the poems in the tradition. The last half of the eighteenth century is saturated with georgics.

Almost any subject was fair game—poets wrote about farming, hunting, manufacturing wool, raising cucumbers, building ships, sailing, preserving health, constructing gardens, and being a village curate, to name but a few topics. Needless to say, a great deal of bad verse was produced. There was also some brilliant humor—Gay's *Trivia* is at once a successful spoof of the tradition and a good comic poem in its own right. If one were to name what have come to be considered the better georgics of the period, one would probably mention *Cyder, Rural Sports, Trivia, A Fragment of a Poem on Hunting, The Chase*, perhaps Armstrong's *The Art of Preserving Health*, Dodsley's *Agriculture*, Dyer's *Fleece*, and Grainger's *Sugar-Cane*. However, with the exception of *Trivia*, one would probably not look for much major poetry in the genre. Thomson's *Seasons* immediately comes to mind as an exception; but that fine poem is only incidentally a georgic, for it combines a vast range of literary and philosophical traditions.

There are several reasons for the georgic tradition's popularity in the eighteenth century. There was the immense prestige of Virgil, but perhaps more important, there was the didactic bent of the age; instruction was popular. There is another reason too, which has to do with the sociological changes occurring in the century. Though the pastoral and the georgic overlap in many respects, the georgic has a much more realistic assessment of rural life. It is next to impossible to write extended, didactic treatments of the activities of humble people without closely sympathizing with them and calling the reader's attention to the idea that humble life *is* important.

This is where one can see a crucial distinction between georgic and pastoral. The pastoral, which has the habit of singing the more pleasant aspects of humble life, uses the rural matter merely for the purposes of objectifying the sophisticated experience of the poet; as one eminent critic states it, pastoral puts "the complex into the simple." In short, whereas the pastoral tradition *looks through* the rural matter, the georgic *looks at* the rural matter. In pastoral, humble life is a *means*; in georgic, an *end*. It is not pastoral but georgic that tends to level social hierarchies and bring all people under the roof of common humanity.

Thus it is not surprising to see that georgics are very strong in the latter part of the period, when the great chain of social levels was breaking down and talk of revolution was in the wind. Some of the poets seemed to be aware of this sociological function of the georgic. Cowper, for example, in Book III of *The Task*, finishes his georgic passage on raising cucumbers with these sentiments:

> Grudge not, ye rich (since luxury must have
> His dainties, and the world's more numerous
>   half
> Lives by contriving delicates for you)
> Grudge not the cost. Ye little know the cares,
> The vigilance, the labour, and the skill,
> That day and night are exercised, and hang
> Upon the ticklish balance of suspense,
> That ye may garnish your profuse regales
> With summer fruits brought forth by
>   wintry suns.

Surely this is not simple pastoral; it is a call, provocative if not revolutionary, for the cultivated readers of Cowper to make room in the world for those at the lower end of the social scale. And though the instructions on raising cucumbers are admittedly a bit ludicrous and tongue-in-cheek, there can be no doubt about the seriousness of the conclusion quoted above.

Elsewhere in this volume, Cowper has been used to illustrate a problem faced by the Augustan poet who had committed himself to a polite level of language but who at the same time had to deal with very low subjects. It needs only to be mentioned here that this problem is especially persistent in the georgic tradition. (See the section dealing with poetic diction, p. 67–68).

Topographical Poem

The topographical poem is a descriptive-reflective work centering around a particular place. One definition maintains that the location must be "specifically named" and "actual"; however, that seems rather artificial. Goldsmith's *Deserted Village*, dealing with fictitious "Auburn," is certainly as realistically rendered as, say, Pope's *Windsor Forest*. And Crabbe's *The Village*, though fictitious, is for most readers much more realistic than the topography of Goldsmith and Pope. Of course, one can do research to find the "sources" of Crabbe and Goldsmith and come to the conclusion that "Auburn" is Lissoy or that Crabbe's town is really Aldborough. But such research finally leads nowhere. It seems acceptable to allow a definition of the topographical

poem to include actual reality and the equally cred-
ible reality created by the poet.

The three chief characteristics of the topographical poem are the fusion of reflection and description,
conciseness, and the interplay of the general and
particular. Such poems were admired for their "incidental meditation," as Johnson said of Denham's
Cooper's Hill, the first bona fide topographical poem.
Another critic, Thomas Paget, praised *Cooper's Hill*
for "the good sense and the fine reflections . . . inter-
woven with the rest."

In addition to fused reflection and description,
the topographical poem had a kind of conciseness
not always apparent in other Augustan genres; this
was due to its habit of attaching itself to a circumscribed locale, which helped to establish
coherence, if not unity. It is useful to compare
Goldsmith's *The Traveller* with his *Deserted Village.*
As the title implies, the former piece meanders,
whereas the *Deserted Village* is probably the most
unified poem that Goldsmith wrote. Still more instructive is a comparison between a thoroughgoing
topographical poem and a piece that, while practic-
ing description and reflection, has not anchored itself to a certain location. For example, Thomson's
The Seasons and Cowper's *The Task* (although each
includes several genres) will immediately appear
diffuse, even though one would not for a moment
deny their passages of great poetry. Sticking to one
locale does not automatically guarantee the unity of
the poem; however, the major works in the topographical tradition have a way of persisting in images relevant to the chosen topography, and thus,
regardless of their themes, they have a kind of built-
in organization.

The interplay of the general and the particular, though it is a process found in virtually all Augustan writing, is especially noteworthy in the topographical genre. Here the poet often creates a kind of tension by resisting the very circumscription that he has assigned to himself. In *Cooper's Hill*, Denham actually says very little about the hill itself. Rather, he spends his lines making observations about the world at large; he sees that St. Paul's in the distance is "Preserved from ruin by the best of kings." In other words, the topographical poet is using his particular hill or forest or village as a means to the end of making general pronouncements—for the Augustan was not especially interested in the unique or the particular. To say, with Denham, that the church is protected by the monarch is to utter a sentiment palatable to many generations of Englishmen. Even the "specific" locales, as handled by the best topographical poets, are generalized. Where exactly is Goldsmith's Deserted Village or Crabbe's Village? Almost anywhere that English culture can be found. And the "order in variety" that Pope saw in Windsor Forest was certainly not peculiar to those woods; his Augustan-Newtonian vision would have spotted these qualities anywhere.

The Augustan topographical tradition, then, generalizes the particular. This is the trend for nearly a century and a half, until we come to the major Romantic poets, who reverse the procedure. Both Wordsworth's "Tintern Abbey" lines and Shelley's use of the "Eugenean Hills" deal not with what these areas mean to all people, but with what the locales mean to themselves. The emphasis has shifted from public to private, from general to particular.

There are any number of poems in English that anticipate the Augustan topographical tradition. Some examples are Marvell's *Upon Appleton House* and Drayton's *Poly Albion*, though the first is too personal (i.e., too particular) and the second too diffuse. The tradition as the eighteenth century was to practice it really begins with Denham, who was, as Johnson commented, "the author of a species of composition that may be denominated *local poetry*" (*Lives of the Poets: Denham*). Then followed Pope's *Windsor Forest*, Dyer's *Grongar Hill*, Goldsmith's *Deserted Village*, and Crabbe's *The Village*. There are literally hundreds of topographical poems in the period, but most of them are of historical rather than literary interest; the great ones are named above. Poets did not limit themselves to hills, forests, and towns, but also wrote about a number of other types of locations, especially rivers and inns.

It may be profitable to end the discussion with a close look at the most imitated and quoted passage in the entire topographical tradition, Denham's famous apostrophe to the Thames in *Cooper's Hill:*

> O could I flow like thee and make thy stream
> My great example, as it is my theme!
> Though deep, yet clear; though gentle, yet
>   not dull,
> Strong without rage, without o'erflowing full.

This is a strong example of the fusing of reflection and description. Throughout the passage the poet is talking simultaneously of the river and of his own character, but it is not by any means a private character. The moderated qualities that Denham seeks are merely the standard of the Golden Mean, which was praised, if not actually striven for, by most Augustans. Similarly, the river is generalized; there are many sizable rivers to which the description would apply. Denham thus brings his character and the river into line with all characters and rivers, reinforcing the eighteenth-century people's love of the expected, the usual, the typical, and hence, the orderly and the stable.

It is interesting to note that the sharp-eyed Dr. Johnson observed that the images "are to be understood simply on one side of the comparison, and metaphorically on the other." That is, the comparison breaks down, perhaps (though Johnson was not specific here) in such expressions as "overflowing" and "full." In what sense can a man's character be said to be "full" or "overflowing"? But Johnson goes on to admire Denham's lines because "so much meaning is comprised in so few words." He liked the topographical poet's conciseness.

Reflective-Descriptive Tradition

The reflective-descriptive poem is a kind of rural topographical poem that has freed itself from its locale. Like the topographical poem, it has no definite pre-Augustan or classical precedent. Also like the topographical piece, it blends reflection with description and concerns itself with the interplay of the general and the particular. But unlike topographical poetry, it is often diffuse and frequently directionless, though neither of these characteristics necessarily makes a bad poem. On the contrary, this rambling, ruminating kind of verse enjoyed a vogue among sophisticated readers through much of the Augustan period, especially after the initial success of Thomson's *The Seasons* in the 1720s. That the tradition continued into the nineteenth century may be seen in Wordsworth's *Prelude* and *Excursion*, both of which are reflective-descriptive poems that have been particularized and individualized in the customary Romantic manner.

In the eighteenth century the two most successful efforts in the tradition are *The Seasons* and Cowper's *The Task*. Other noteworthy attempts are Anne Finch's *Nocturnal Reverie* (a quasi-graveyard poem), Pomfret's *The Choice*, Green's *The Spleen*, and Falconer's *The Shipwreck*. The last two represent the ends of a spectrum, for *The Spleen* leans heavily on reflection while *The Shipwreck* is mostly description. One of the best efforts came at the very end, in 1810, when the late-Augustan George Crabbe beautifully balanced reflection and description in his *The Borough*. (Though confined to one area of England, *The Borough* covers too much territory— physically and spiritually—to be judged a true topographical poem.)

As implied above, the reflective-descriptive poem was sometimes almost militantly diffuse. The idea was not to stay on a particular topic, theme, or image, but rather to wander freely about. It may have been this studied carelessness that caused Dr. Johnson to complain that "the great defect of *The Seasons* is want of method." However, he went on to say, "for this I know not that there was any remedy. Of many appearances subsisting all at once, no rule can be given why one should be mentioned before another." Even so, Johnson maintained, the problem in reading *The Seasons* is that "the memory wants the help of order, and the curiosity is not excited by suspense or expectation" [*Lives of the Poets: Thomson*].

Perhaps Johnson's mixed reaction to Thomson's poem can serve as a *caveat* to modern readers. It is a violation of the spirit of the reflective-descriptive tradition to search for "structure" or "unity" in these poems, for that is the very thing that they are trying to avoid. With the present-day fascination with "unity" or "functional form," many a modern critic has been led astray in the thickets and meanderings of poets like Thomson and Cowper. An accurate sense of the diffusion of the tradition may be gained by glancing at the table of contents for Book I of Cowper's *The Task:*

Historical deduction of seats, from the stool to the sofa—A school-boy's ramble—A walk in the country—The scene described—Rural sounds as well as sights delightful—Another walk—Mistake concerning the charms of solitude, corrected—Colonnades commended—Alcove and the view from it—The Wilderness—The grove—The thresher—The necessity and the benefits of exercise—The works of nature superior to and in some ways inimitable by art—The wearisomeness of what is commonly called a life of pleasure—Change of scene sometimes expedient—A common described, and the character of Crazy Kate introduced upon it—Gipsies—The blessings of civilized life—That state most favorable to virtue—The South Sea Islanders compassionated, but chiefly Omai—His present

state of mind supposed—Civilized life friendly
to virtue, but not great cities—Great cities, and
London in particular, allowed their due praise,
but censured—Fête champêtre—The book concludes with a reflection on the fatal effects of dis-
sipation and effeminacy upon our public
measures.

This is a wonderfully relaxed state of affairs, inviting
the reader to be at ease, enjoying himself and tarry-
ing along the way. There can be no hurry to get to
the end when the poem cannot even be said to have
one.

Because the nature of the reflective-descriptive
tradition is an encyclopedic all-inclusiveness, it cannot be defined on the basis of subject matter.
However, some of the favorite topics were: nature
(e.g., description of the change of seasons); trade and
commerce; the military; rural occupations; social
reform; politics; history; literary history and criticism; the evils of the city and the goodness of the
country (though no reflective-descriptive poet was
so naive as to take a completely pastoral view of the
country); death and immortality; praise of friends or
celebrities; occasional satire; manners and customs
of foreign countries; superstition; science; and—quite
important—the Horatian ideal of cultured rural
retirement.

The point is not that the reflective-descriptive
poets had a monopoly on the above-mentioned
topics—one could find many of them in a straight
topographical poem—it is just that poems like *The
Seasons* and *The Task* have a greater persistent
wealth of topics than any other type of Augustan

verse. It is this abundance of topics that makes one refrain from calling reflective-descriptive poetry a "genre," for in reality it is many genres in one. Within the broad and comfortable confines of *The Seasons,* the reader can find passages of georgic, pastoral, topographical, and graveyard poetry, epigram, Juvenalian and Horatian satire, elegy, and any number of others. One critic has said that Thomson thought "knowledge" was "art" and thus loaded his poem with everything he knew. But it may be just as accurate to say that, like a number of his fellow reflective-descriptive poets, Thomson felt that art was genres.

"Graveyard School"

The "graveyard poem" or "night piece" of the eighteenth century does not constitute a sharply defined genre, but there are enough major poems of this sort to allow one to make some useful generalizations. A graveyard poem is a work, usually in blank verse or some form other than the heroic couplet (e.g., the heroic or elegaic stanzas of Gray's *Elegy Written in a Country Churchyard*), which in most instances has eight main objectives.

First, it reminds the reader in no uncertain terms that he must eventually die. Though few readers need such reminding, the graveyard poet has a way of bludgeoning one with this melancholy realization: " 'Think, mortal, what it is to die!' " shout the ghosts rising from tombs in Parnell's *A Night-Piece on Death.*

Second, such poetry has an objective of discoursing, frequently at some length, upon the vanity and transitoriness of life, a theme that can be said to be central to Gray's *Elegy*.

Another objective of the graveyardist (if one may coin a term) is to create and then build upon a setting of nighttime in a place of burial, usually a churchyard or a crypt; many of the graveyard poems open with the sun just setting or having set over the graves.

A fourth desire of the poet is to deal with physical decay after death. Probably the most strenuous here is Robert Blair, whose work *The Grave* lavishes much description on the "blank" faces of corpses and on the vaults that are "Furred round with mouldy damps and ropy slime."

Fifth, the graveyardist invariably suggests that Death is the leveler, an idea popular throughout the seventeenth century and just as popular in the eighteenth. Death obliterates all social distinctions, and even sceptre and crown must come tumbling down.

The sixth graveyard poem objective is to adopt and maintain an exceedingly gloomy and funereal tone. Sometimes, when the poet is not quite up to the task, the tone gets out of control so that one encounters, for example, the unintentional humor of Blair. He addresses a deceased surgeon with this sarcasm:

Tell us, thou doughty keeper from the grave,
Where are thy recipes and cordials now...?

The gloomy tone is established by a certain stock imagery or diction that is found throughout the graveyard tradition. *Dim, melancholy, livid, solemn, crumbled, shades, shrouds, bones, parting, silent*— these and dozens of similar words bulk large in the vocabulary of this poetry. They make up a minor part of standard Augustan poetic diction (discussed below).

As a seventh discernible objective, the poem, in spite of its melancholy gloom, ultimately moves toward some sort of reconciliation, usually Christian, with the fact of death, so that the hideous prospect of physical decay becomes a mere transitional state through which one must pass on his way to the glories of the afterlife. However, no skillful graveyardist lets his reader off the hook of morbidity until the very last minute. The objective is more to make us indulge ourselves in thoughts of death than to reveal to us the hope of salvation. An analogy to this procedure might be the prurient Restoration comedy, which, after four and three-fourths acts of unapologetic bawdiness, tacks on a moral at the end.

Finally, the eighth objective of the graveyard poem is to emphasize the solitude of the speaker, usually in hopes that his loneliness, together with the night-in-the-charnel-house type of setting, will throw the reader into a mood of profound depression.

The above, then, are the chief ingredients of the graveyard poem; however, they do not necessarily take shape in the order described here in the individual works. Indeed, except for the tendency to make peace with death at the end, the tradition allows itself a fairly loose kind of structure. It is ruminative and digressive, perhaps like the state of mind of a person sicklied o'er with the pale cast of thinking about death and the brevity of life.

There are many thoroughgoing graveyard pieces in the eighteenth century, but only four can be considered major: Parnell's *A Night-Piece on Death*; Young's *Night Thoughts*; Blair's *The Grave*; and of course Gray's *Elegy*. Other successful poems may be considered either genuine graveyard pieces or close relations to the tradition: Ann Finch's *Nocturnal Reverie*; Gay's *Contemplation on Night*; some of Shenstone's *Elegies*; and, to go on to the second half of the century, Beattie's *Elegy, Written in the Year 1758*; Edward Moore's *An Elegy Written Among the Ruins of a Nobleman's Seat in Cornwall*; and John Cunningham's *An Elegy on a Pile of Ruins*. As is suggested by the titles, Gray's *Elegy* had a far-reaching influence. One of the best imitators was Richard Jago, whose *An Elegy on Man* is at once good Gray and good graveyard: "Forever now to be forgot, / Amid the mouldering clay." There are also many poems that, though they belong to the much *wider* tradition of general melancholy, do not share the specific, grim focus of the true graveyardist.

What is interesting to note is that the major and famous graveyard poems of Parnell, Young, Blair, and Gray appear in the first half of the century (Gray's *Elegy*, published in 1751, was probably begun in 1742). One would at first tend to think that it should be the other way around, for it is the second half of the century that readers have come to associate with the kind of sensibility displayed by the graveyardist. But there are several good reasons why the first half of the 1700s should see graveyardism in full flower. For one thing, this genre, like satire and the ode, could provide the poet with an escape from restraint; the unbridled effusions of the graveyardist would have little place in most of the Augustan genres.

Another possibility is that writers saw the graveyard poem as a way of declaring independence from the ancients. Here was a kind of writing that seemed to have no genuine classical model (except for parts of Lucretius' *On the Nature of Things*), a kind of writing that put the Augustan on his own. One is reminded here of the paradox that to be like the ancients is to be unlike them — that is, *original*. This intriguing contradiction was pointed out in *Conjectures on Original Composition*, written by the half-Augustan, half-graveyardist Edward Young.

Again, it should be noted that melancholy per se was popular in the first half of the century, partly due to the taste of the middle class, which since the Glorious Revolution of 1688–1689 had been growing increasingly louder in its demands for an active role in English culture. In any case, there was a small proliferation of manuals dealing with the art of meditation. Two of the best-known were Mrs. Elizabeth Rowe's *Friendship in Death* (1728) and James Hervey's *Meditation Among the Tombs* (1746), which was later rendered into blank verse. Thus the graveyard poet was in a sense merely putting a middle-class fashion into a poetic form. Interestingly enough, although the best graveyard poems might be for the most part written by gentlemen of the upper classes, they appealed to the middle class, which found such sentiments as death-as-leveler exceedingly congenial. Though it would be reckless to argue that the graveyardist was instrumental in breaking down the social hierarchy, it is safe to say that he could easily be seen as one who in a modest way anticipated the new society that was to form by the end of the century.

The above, then, are some of the possible reasons for the great "graveyard activity" during the early eighteenth century. It only remains to say a word about the history of the genre. "Word" is used advisedly, for there is no real development of the tradition prior to the Augustan Age. Though it may not spring fully grown from the mind of the eighteenth-century individual, it is not until this period that one can find a thoroughgoing graveyard poem. Before the eighteenth century, if one excludes certain funeral elegies and such pieces as the *Emblems* of Thomas Quarles, there is very little in literature to foreshadow definitely the specific work of Thomas Gray and his group. And by the close of the Augustan period there is—fortunately or unfortunately, depending on one's tastes—very little significant production of the poetry of sustained night thoughts in churchyards.

Poetic Diction

The poetic diction of the eighteenth century consists of personifications, Latinisms, certain stock words or phrases, y-ending adjectives, periphrasis or circumlocution, occasional pagan deities, and a particular use of the article *the*. Though it is found most often in poetry that describes nature—especially the georgic and pastoral traditions—it is fairly widespread in all of the poetic kinds of the period.

A thorough history of poetic diction would have to begin virtually with the beginning of literature itself, for every age has its poetic diction, including the present. Certain images or constructions used dazzlingly by such influential writers as T. S. Eliot or

Dylan Thomas have a way of turning up in the poetry of later writers. The diction of the age thus becomes solidified, only to be vigorously attacked and discarded by the following age, which in turn creates its own diction.

But in the eighteenth century the poetic diction was more sharply defined than in the preceding or succeeding periods. There was a relatively stable social structure that resulted in a definite community of agreement between readers and writers. There were certain assumptions about levels of style that were shared by all those involved in the literary world. And there was a strong sense of propriety and decorum in the polite use of language.

A history of the poetic diction of the eighteenth century can properly begin in the English Renaissance. All of the devices listed in the definition above can be found in Milton and, to a lesser degree, in Shakespeare and Spenser. It is accurate to say that these poets enjoyed a fairly consistent prestige in the Augustan Age, provided one stresses that they were a little more popular later in the period and that they tended to be more prestigious among the *young poets just beginning their careers.* Many a young Augustan came under the spell of the English Masters when at a very impressionable age.

Milton, Shakespeare, and Spenser were not of course the only sources of poetic diction. The heaviest pre-Augustan concentration of such language appears in a minor writer, Joshua Sylvester, who, around the turn of the sixteenth-seventeenth centuries, was translating Du Bartas's long poem on the Creation and the history of humankind. Much of the poetic diction in Sylvester was a rendering of the original, but the translator added some of his own. In the meantime, the ever-growing prestige of the ancient Romans ensured that Virgil and, to a lesser degree, Ovid would also be influential in the growth of poetic diction. Indeed, a great number of the favorite Latinisms of the eighteenth century come directly from the *Georgics*—"liquid," "invade," and "refulgent," for example.

During the period extending from just before the Restoration to the end of the seventeenth century, the growth of poetic diction was temporarily slackened. The chief reason was the New Science, which had the effect of demanding a "plain" sort of writing and excluding "flowery language." But poetic diction from Sylvester to Cowper is never really totally eclipsed. It took the Romantic poets to all but do away with it. And honesty would admit that, like all literary movements and styles, poetic diction had finally gone to seed in a shabby ludicrousness such as that in the nature descriptions of Erasmus Darwin—just as the metaphysical poetry had gone to seed in Cleveland and in the less successful poems of Crashaw. Honesty would also admit that, in spite of their strictures against Augustan poetic diction, the Romantics occasionally made magnificent use of it. There are, for example, some fine personifications in Keats.

Any treatment of poetic diction would do well to begin with personification, for it is probably one of the least understood and most interesting devices in this period. Strictly speaking, personification occurs when an abstract idea is given a human characteristic: "Reason frowns on War's unequal game" (Johnson's *Vanity of Human Wishes*). But occasionally personifications can involve a material thing, as in Pope's *Eloisa to Abelard* in which there is the expression "relentless walls." The personified abstraction has been praised by recent critics for its function of uniting the general with the particular and the abstract with the concrete. Much of the praise is justified, but it should be pointed out that the general and the abstract were much less vague or hazy to the eighteenth century than to the twentieth century. Such popular Augustan concepts as "virtue," "crime," "reason," and "folly" had particular meanings for the closely integrated eighteenth-century world of letters, in which the poet was on familiar terms with a relatively small audience. Thus the personification is often less a matter of yoking together opposites than a matter of the Augustan poet exploiting the stabilized attitudes of his audience.

Recent criticism has also approached personification from the point of view of the "allegorical" and the "metaphorical." Generally speaking, the allegorical personification is static and more pictorial, while the metaphorical is dynamic and tries to dramatize a moral or philosophical truth. Johnson's "Reason frowns," mentioned above, would be allegorical, whereas this couplet from Johnson's *The Ant* would be metaphorical:

Till Want, now following fraudulent and slow,
Shall spring to seize thee like an ambushed foe.

Another Johnsonian example of dynamic personification occurs in *London:* "Slow rises Worth, by Poverty depressed." If there is excitement in this famous line, it probably derives not only from the personifications themselves but also from the pressure of the syntax, which suspensefully withholds the relationship between worth and poverty until the very last word: *depressed.*

Though a master of personification, Johnson is not of course the only successful user of this device. From the 1740s until the close of the eighteenth century, it is widespread in English poetry, becoming especially strong in the ode. Two reasons for its prevalence in the ode are that this genre was associated with wildness or emotion—as was personification—and that the ode was highly pictorial and thus suited to personification, which is almost always a visual figure. Indeed, some odes—Collins's *Pity* and *Fear*, for example—are constructed around single extended personifications.

Because the twentieth century is still laboring somewhat under the stigma the Romantics placed upon personification, the best way for the modern reader to approach the figure is to have an open and sympathetic attitude and to keep in mind that the personification to the Augustans could be as exciting as such concepts or techniques as *die Angst* or "ambivalence" are exciting to the present age. If one might bring in Johnson again, it is revealing to notice that in his *Vanity of Human Wishes* the personifications are thickest in the section dealing with the plight of the scholar. This is not surprising, for the human wish of scholarly achievement was dearest to the great lexicographer's heart. In short, Johnson was at his most emotional here, and he chose one of the favorite Augustan devices for showing emotion—personification.

Latinisms, another element in poetic diction,

were widely used throughout the eighteenth century. One apparent reason for their popularity in the period was the prestige of the classical writers and the related feeling that English, as a new and "vulgar" tongue, needed the support of the older language. But in taking Latin words into English the poet could enjoy an automatic double entendre (the Latin meaning and the English) and thus transcend the classical authors. There are some magnificent examples in *Paradise Lost*, though in Milton the definition is often slightly more Latin than English.

The best Augustans, however, could frequently use the Latin word so that *both* its English and original meanings had great force. An interesting example occurs in the *Nocturnal Reverie* of Ann Finch, a minor though very skillful poetess. She writes that the soul soaring in reverie "Joys in the inferior world, and thinks it like her own." "Inferior" originally meant *lower*, but the context obviously demands also the English definition of *reduced status* or *lack of value*. Once in a while eighteenth-century poets use the interplay between Latin and English to redefine words and thus breathe new life into them. In George Crabbe's *The Borough*, Letter XXIII, there is an attack on the debtors "who mean to live / On credit, that credulity will give." The juxtaposing of "credit" and "credulity" reminds the reader of the Latin force of the root *cred*, which has to do with faith, trust, and honesty, rather than with cold and impersonal business transactions. The total effect is to refreshen the language and remind us of our responsibilities as moral human beings.

Certain stock words or phrases in poetic diction have long been a cause of adverse criticism of the eighteenth-century poet. Readers have had the feeling that the Augustans were too lazy or unoriginal to think of something new and consequently fell back on a cheap, ready-made vocabulary. There is some truth to this charge, especially when brought against the "decadents" at the end of the period. But a defense of the Augustans is that they often put more value on the *new use of the old*, the successful exploitation of the tried and true, than on the totally new. Eighteenth-century readers set great value on recognition, not on being tantalizingly baffled by the totally new. Moreover, many of the stock words or phrases had a function that may escape the notice of readers who lack sympathy for the world views of the period.

Each of the above points may be illustrated by long-famous expressions widely used in eighteenth-century verse. The new use of the old can be seen in Pope's description of shepherds who each morning "Poured over the whitening vale their fleecy care" *(Pastorals: Spring)*. One recent critic explains that "whitening" was used by Virgil *(Aeneid,* Book IV) to mean the dawn illuminating the valley, and that Pope has retained this meaning but added the new meaning of the *sheep* whitening the vale. Interestingly enough, Pope's cleverness encouraged Shenstone and Cowper to use similar images; thus the evolution of the expression moves from the old, to a new use of the old, and then back to the no-longer-new.

That the stock phrases or words had meaning relevant to the Augustans and irrelevant to many modern readers can be seen in "the wandering moon," an expression which occurs frequently not only in the Augustans but in the Renaissance writers as well. Its function was not merely to lie inert as dead language but to help classify and place the moon and thus reaffirm the order and harmony in the divine scheme of things. The moon "wanders" in the sense that, unlike the fixed heavenly bodies, it appears to the earthbound observer to have an unsteady and wandering course. "That is what the moon does; that is its function," this diction seems to imply; "there is order and purpose in the cosmos." A shrewd variation on this image occurs in Ann Finch's *Nocturnal Reverie:*

> When in some river overhung with green,
> The waving moon and trembling leaves
>   are seen.

Without discarding the old image of the moon wandering in the sky, the poet has added the new one of the moon's reflection in the rippling water.

Adjectives that end in y are a common ingredient of poetic diction. There are any number of them in Spenser, Shakespeare, and Milton, and they are especially concentrated in Sylvester's rendering of Du Bartas. In the Augustan period they are prominent in nature description, though one can find them in all poets of the century. Like the stock words and phrases, they frequently have the function of classifying and placing things in the cosmos. For almost two hundred years, fish were often referred to as "finny," as in "the finny breed," "the finny kind," "the finny tribe," etc. Such an expression unites the particular with the general, for though there are numerous "breeds," only one of them is "finny." This may be laboring the obvious, but the Augustan readers enjoyed again and again seeing the order and harmony of the universe reaffirmed; they delighted in a sense of certainty. They knew of course that fish were the only *finny* breed, but they loved to hear it eloquently reasserted.

It is also worth mentioning that scientists were assiduously classifying empirical reality, and the y-adjective lent itself admirably to a careful and orderly description of nature; such adjectives are numerous in the scientific writings of the period. By using them the poet could invoke the prestige of science and at the same time avail himself of an accurate and serviceable vocabulary. It is ironic that the New Science of the Restoration should have discouraged the growth of poetic diction, because by the late 1700s, science was to become a major aid in the writing of verse.

The chief reason the Augustans turned to circumlocution, a major part of poetic diction, was their great concern with levels of style and propriety in the choice of words. The age had a strong sense of the just and appropriate, which can be epitomized with Swift's definition of good style as "proper words in proper places." Further, the eighteenth-century poets felt that unless specific purposes of humor or satire called for it, language should maintain a polite level at all times—polite but not necessarily stuffy or pompous.

This attitude created problems. What was the serious writer to do when his subject was low? If he maintained a high level of diction, his work would immediately appear silly; on the other hand, vulgar or common language would not do. A rather brilliant, if somewhat tongue-in-cheek solution to this problem turns up in Book III of Cowper's *The Task.* The poet wants to tell his readers about the art of raising cucumbers in a greenhouse, and yet he has previously committed himself to writing in stately blank verse. Cowper's solution is to approach his humble subject matter in a high style and then let the language descend gradually until it matches the subject. Such items as manure and the cucumber itself are at first referred to as the "stercoraceous mass" and the "prickly and green-coated gourd." Then the style gradually moves down until the specific words "manure" and "cucumber" are used—but not until a number of lines of preparation have gone by.

Incidentally, Cowper's problem is one that frequently occurs in the georgic, a genre which characteristically calls for a humble subject usually having to do with agriculture or the manual arts. Virgil was the great model here, for as Addison had said years before Cowper wrote, the classical poet had the ability to "toss the dung about with an air of gracefulness." No less ludicrous is the incident related in Boswell's *Life of Johnson* in which the poet James Grainger was laughed out of the room with his line "Now, Muse, let's sing of rats." Later he changed it to "the whiskered vermin race," though Boswell still disliked it—suggesting that in the Augustan Age the demand was for skillful periphrasis and that not just any circumlocution would do.

The above, then, are some of the problems encountered by poets who had committed themselves to a polite standard of diction. Though such a commitment could make fools of many writers, it also posed wonderful possibilities for sometimes breath-taking ascents or descents in the level of style. It also presented large opportunities for humor, specifically in the mock-heroic or burlesque.

Pagan deities are sometimes a part of eighteenth-century poetic diction, but even though it was an age of neoclassicism, there is far less mythology in the poetry than one might expect. On the other hand, it has often been pointed out that pagan mythology was absorbed by Augustan schoolchildren from their basic texts and that in most polite houses there were any number of statues or paintings of the Greek and Roman gods and heroes. With this kind of saturation, it is not surprising that some mythology should creep into the poetry. But compared to the English Renaissance there is relatively little use of pagan deities in the verse of the eighteenth century. When they do appear, they have about them an air of fatigue and overuse: "And reddening Phoebus lifts his golden fire," a line from a sonnet by Gray, was justly condemned by the Romantics.

The article *the* is not a very important part of poetic diction, but it is mentioned here because in Augustan verse it has a function not often noticed by the modern reader. It lends an air of familiarity to what is *already familiar.* That is, Augustan readers enjoyed recognizing the familiar aspects of their cosmos and social environment; they were not interested in the highly particular or unique. If the poet wrote that a rustic gave "*a* long loud laugh, sincere," the article *a* would have a way of singling out this laugh and over-particularizing—that would not do in an age that loved the general and the universal. Thomson's *Seasons (Winter),* from which the line is paraphrased, actually reads "*the* long loud laugh, sincere," which elicits a response to this effect: "Yes, there is the familiar rustic whom we have seen many times before." The same point can be made about the plight of the scholar in Johnson's *The Vanity of Human Wishes:*

> There mark what ills *the* scholar's life assail,
> Toil, envy, want, *the* patron, and *the* jail.
> [my italics]

Patrons and prisons are all-too-familiar aspects of the Augustan's literary experience.

Augustan poetic diction can be excellent or execrable, depending on how the poet uses it. However that may be, it is in and through the countryside of eighteenth-century verse.

III

The Augustan "Lyric"

This chapter deals with the ode, song, hymn, sonnet, ballad, Anacreontic, and elegy—in that
order. Though all of these might be classified as
lyrics, a *genuine* lyric is rare in the eighteenth century, for the period set little value on the strenuous
expression of personal emotion—"the spontaneous
overflow of powerful feelings." Instead, the eighteenth-century writer imposed on himself a doctrine
of restraint; therefore the above-mentioned poetic
forms tended to be public and universal rather than
private and individual. There are strong feelings in
Augustan lyrics, especially in the ode, but those feelings are controlled, if not actually repressed, by
being generalized and standardized. It is instructive
to compare an Augustan lyric like Gray's *Ode on a
Distant Prospect of Eton College* with a Romantic
piece like Coleridge's *Dejection: An Ode.* One immediately notices the general application of Gray
("Where ignorance is bliss, / 'Tis folly to be wise") as
opposed to the intense privacy and personal feeling
of Coleridge.

71

Ode

A popular definition of the ode is that it is an ex-
alted, lyrical address to a person or object of dignity—but there are comic odes too. In its widest
sense, an ode can be any sort of lyric using virtually
any kind of meter, stanza, and rhyme form. As can
be seen in the derivation of the word ("song"), the
ode is frequently associated with music, though at
least by the middle of the eighteenth century it
becomes poetry in its own right.

The ode began in ancient Greece with Pindar
whose works celebrate athletic heroes whom the
poet often associates with the gods. The other major
classical writer of odes, as far as the Augustans were
concerned, was the ancient Roman Horace, whose
work shows more restraint than Pindar's. Horace's
odes celebrate morality, love, and patriotism, and are
simpler in form than those of his Greek counterpart.

Like most of the classical forms, the ode went underground in the medieval period, after which it
emerged in the Renaissance under the auspices of
Ronsard, who in the sixteenth century helped to
revive Pindar as a great name and a proper model in
the writing of odes. Englishmen of the Elizabethan
Age wrote odes, but their primary interests lay in
other forms. Early in the seventeenth century, the
feeling that the Psalms of David were odes lent much
prestige to the genre. From this point on, the ode was
established in English literature. It was used for en-
comiums at court and at the universities; and when
Milton composed his ode *On the Morning of Christ'*
Nativity, he knew he had chosen a type of poem suffi-
ciently dignified for his subject.

As the seventeenth century progressed, there was a growing tendency to associate the ode with wildness or lack of restraint, as can be seen in Crashaw and Cowley. Thus it is not surprising to see that by the time of the Restoration the ode was being used by Samuel Butler, John Oldham, and others for coarse, rough satire. However, the form retained both its association with music and its air of dignity, as is evident in the numerous odes to Saint Cecelia (patron saint of music) of the late seventeenth century.

Dryden was one of the better pioneers of the ode. He was instrumental in smoothing out the wildness of Cowley and Crashaw (though the ode never entirely lost its atmosphere of escaping from restraint). Because he was successful in his odes on *Alexander's Feast* and *Anne Killigrew*, later writers were willing to be influenced by him.

In the early eighteenth century the ode began to dissolve its long partnership with music, but it remained hospitable to religion, as in the odes of Isaac Watts. The mid-eighteenth century saw the great "Pindaric revival" in the poetry of Gray and Collins and, with less success, in the Wartons, Shenstone, and Akenside. But in an age of restraint, the somewhat uninhibited ode was still suspect, as evidenced by Johnson's attack upon Gray's *The Bard* (*Lives of the Poets*).

The later eighteenth century is not famous for its odes, but some important developments did take place. Burns, Grainger, Beattie, and Mason exploited the form to make it, if not wilder than before, at least more personal, thus preparing the way for the intensely personal note in Wordsworth's *Ode on the In-*

timations of Immortality or in the great odes of Keats. The minor poets of the late Augustan Age were also involved in trimming down some of the poetic diction that admittedly had gotten somewhat out of hand in the Pindaric revival of the mid-century. The very late eighteenth-century writers also made the ode move towards the philosophical and away from the purely emotional. But in the Augustan Age, the ode never lost its less serious side. There were a number of satirical odes produced in the period, the most famous of which is Gray's *Ode on the Death of a Favourite Cat,* and late in the century "Peter Pindar" (John Wolcot) published a number of mock-odes.

As mentioned earlier, the ode is elusive of definition. Nevertheless, one can discern several general categories. The Pindaric or regular ode uses the traditional strophe, antistrophe, and epode derived from the movements of the chorus in ancient Greek drama. Writers of this type of ode usually felt that the strophe and antistrophe ought to be in the same stanza form but that the epode could use a different sort of stanza. Once this pattern was established, however, it was considered inappropriate to alter it; on the other hand, one could have as many *sets* of strophe, antistrophe, and epode as he wished. With apologies to Dr. Johnson, Gray's *The Bard* is a good example of a Pindaric or regular ode.

A second major type of ode, popular not only in the Augustan Age but in the periods before and after the eighteenth century, was the Horatian or homostrophic ode. This was a more Spartan kind of poem that allowed itself only one stanza form. The influence of Horace dictated that the stanzas should usually have four lines (as in Johnson's translations

of Horace's odes), though this was not always practiced. Three examples—before, during, and after the
Augustan Age—are Andrew Marvell's *Horatian Ode
upon Cromwell's Return from Ireland,* Thomas Tickell's *Ode, Occasioned By His Excellency the Earl of
Stanhope's Voyage to France,* and Coleridge's *Ode to
France.* It could be safely generalized that the Horatian ode exhibits more restraint than the Pindaric or
regular ode.

A third type of ode practiced in the Augustan
Age is the irregular ode, which, as the name implies,
allows complete freedom in the arrangement of
either strophes or stanza forms; it has no consistency
of outward form. Cowley is chiefly responsible for
getting the irregular ode started. (Incidentally, the
story that Cowley used such undisciplined forms in
the belief that he was writing Pindarics has long
since been discredited.) Dryden's great *Alexander's
Feast* is a good example of an irregular ode (though
Dryden would have called it a Pindaric). Another
very respectable example later on in the period is
Shenstone's *An Irregular Ode After Sickness.*

The Augustan ode may be classified by two
other schemes that cut across the preceding categories. It may be grouped according to seriousness of
intent; that is, broken down into mock-or-comic-odes
(Gray's ode on the cat) and the serious odes (all of
Collins's odes). A more significant scheme is to divide the ode into categories of sublime and beautiful.
The sublime is associated with the astounding, the
transporting, the vast, and the astonishing, as in
Gray's *The Bard.* The beautiful (i.e., neat, orderly,
pretty, pleasing) might be discerned in Gray's carefully controlled *Ode on a Distant Prospect of Eton Col-*

lege. The mid-century poets also talked about categories of "descriptive" and "allegorical" odes, but the two are often fused because they are both highly pictorial, a characteristic of virtually any ode.

That the ode, a genre that admits freedom and wildness, should be popular in an age of restraint is not surprising. People need their safety valves, and when the ostensible lyric had gone underground the ode emerged as an avenue of escape. It was a poet's poem, and even the more decorous of Augustans could have a recess from regimen in the genre. It is symptomatic that even Johnson followed suit, in his fairly exuberant *An Ode on Friendship:*

> When virtues kindred virtues meet,
> And sister souls together join,
> Thy pleasures, permanent as great
> Are all transporting, all divine.
>
> Oh, must their ardors cease to glow
> When souls to blissful climes remove?
> What raised our virtues here below,
> Shall aid our happiness above.

This passage would seem to indicate that the normally restrained Johnson could allow himself to be a little more emotional in this genre.

Song

The Augustan song is a short poem, frequently composed in quatrains, sometimes written for musical accompaniment, and engineered for the most part to come as close as possible to lyric without actually being a lyric. At the risk of an oversimplification, one might generalize that whereas the eighteenth century song sings of "how one feels about it," the true lyric sings of "how *I* feel about it." What is usually lacking in the Augustan song is the genuinely personal note. But there is nothing inherently valuable about the distinctly personal note, and it is certainly true that the period produced a great number of first-rate songs.

To name the poets of the Augustan Age who wrote at least one successful song would be to draw up a list of practically every poet in the period. One may, however, offer some short groupings of the more successful miners of this vein. In the Restoration or the late seventeenth century, there is some beautiful work by Edmund Waller, Dryden, Sir Charles Sedley, Sir George Etherege, Charles Sackville (Earl of Dorset), John Wilmot (Earl of Rochester), Thomas Flatman, Thomas D'Urfey, Robert Gould, and Philip Ayres. Of this late-seventeenth-century group, the most brilliant, if not the most prolific, was Edmund Waller, whose *Go Lovely Rose* was echoed throughout the eighteenth century and is even today a frequently anthologized classic.

In the earlier eighteenth century the song tradition persisted, though by this time it had lost some of its close association with music. Some of the better song writers were George Granville (who could also be considered late-seventeenth-century), William Congreve, Ambrose Philips, John Gay, Matthew Prior, Thomas Parnell, and George Lyttelton (Baron Lyttelton).

In the later eighteenth century, one cannot omit Blake from this list, even though this poet is well outside the Augustan mainstream. Other successful song writers were Robert Burns, Thomas Chatterton, Oliver Goldsmith, Christopher Smart, and James Beattie. There were also those writers who are chiefly known for their writing in other genres but who are also known for one famous song—for example, James Thomson *(Rule Britannia)* and Henry Fielding *(The Roast Beef of Old England)*.

One danger in discussing a genre so prolific as the song is that there is a tendency to fall into a monotonous pattern of naming names, subjects, or types—and the present writer is well aware that he has already sinned on this head in the above lists. However, there seems to be no other way out, especially if one wants to give a just representation of the fecundity of the song. With this in mind, then, the discussion will move on to consider varieties of subject matter.

One critic, who, though she purports to discuss the lyric, is actually discussing the song, sees five main categories of topics in the Augustan song: unrequited love; carpe diem (literally "seize the day," the subject of Waller's *Go Lovely Rose*); woman's power over her lover; the fickle woman; and an "Ovidian" group exhibiting a rather cynical approach to love. Since this critic has restricted herself to love, one might add other categories: songs of conviviality; of sport; of patriotism; and of the sea. The point would seem to be that the song takes all of experience for its province; there are no boundaries, and anything is a potential song.

As far as tone is concerned, an eighteenth-century song may range from the rowdy scurrility of the bawdyhouse to the porcelain polish of the court. Rochester was notorious for certain lewd songs,

some of which are almost printable. Here is one,
quoted in full:

> Love a woman! y'are an ass,
> 'Tis a most insipid passion,
> To choose out for your happiness!
> The idlest part of God's Creation.
>
> Let the porter, and the groom,
> Things designed for dirty slaves,
> Drudge in fair Aurelia's womb
> To get supplies for age, and graves.
>
> Farewell woman, I intend,
> Henceforth, every night to sit,
> With my lewd well-natured friend,
> Drinking, to engender wit.
>
> Then give me health, wealth, mirth,
>   and wine,
> And if busie love intrenches,
> There's a sweet soft page of mine,
> Does the trick worth forty wenches.

Compared to some others of Rochester, it is spotless.
Yet the same poet could write *Love and Life*, easily
one of the most perfect songs in the entire Augustan
period, quoted here in full:

> All my past life is mine no more,
> The flying hours are gone;
> Like transitory dreams given o'er,
> Whose images are kept in store,
> By memory alone.
>
> Whatever is to come, is not,

How can it then be mine?
The present moment's all my lot,
And that as fast as it is got,
Phillis, is wholly thine.

Then talk not of inconstancy,
False hearts and broken vows,
If I by miracle can be
This live-long minute true to thee,
'Tis all that Heaven allows.

It is this infinite variety in subject matter, meter, and tone that makes any discussion of the song necessarily inconclusive. Still it is accurate to say that the song comes close to forming a genre of its own; on one side, it shades off into the genuine, truly personal lyric, and on the other side, it shades off into the ballad and hymn.

While mentioning lyric, it might be well to notice that Rochester's *Love and Life* is, in spite of its beauty, nothing more than rather standard cavalier expression and sentiment. It is not Vaughan's "I saw eternity the other night" nor is it Wordsworth's "I wandered lonely as a cloud." Rather, Rochester belongs in that long tradition of the impersonal song that spans the period from the Metaphysical to the Romantic.

As implied in the previous paragraph, the Augustan song owes something to the cavalier tradition—e.g., Lovelace, Suckling, Herrick, Carew. But it would be wrong to say that this is the only source. The Augustans knew the ancients, who had written many a porcelain lyric (e.g., Horace) and had thus furnished some precedent for the song in the neoclassical age. Another source was the great interest in music in the later seventeenth century, when Samuel Pepys and his friends got together to sing and when Saint Cecelia, patron saint of music, was honored everywhere. Then, too, there was the familiar "broadside" or street ballad, often written to be sung and frequently constructed around an actual happening such as an execution or a fire. And finally one might maintain that the impulse toward song writing is one that is present in every age; thus it is not surprising to find it in the eighteenth century. Nor is it surprising to see that the Augustans gave the song their own definite touch, keeping it impersonal, often polished, and frequently exquisite.

Hymn

In modern English literature there are several traditions of religious verse, ranging from the complex intellectuality of the Metaphysical poets, or of such poetic treatises as Spenser's *Four Hymns* and Sir John Davies's *Nosce Teipsum,* to the simpler efforts that one sees in versified psalms and in standard hymns. Only the standard hymn is involved in the present discussion, for it is in this area that the eighteenth century made its greatest contribution to religious poetry.

The word *hymn* derives ultimately from the Greek *hymnos,* meaning "song" or "ode." Thus it can be observed that Isaac Watts, one of the two greatest hymnists of the period, sometimes refers to his religious pieces as odes. Indeed, there are also a number of areas in which the song and the hymn shade off into each other. Nevertheless, one can bring forth a fairly specific working definition of the hymn: It is a short poem in simple language, usually intended to be sung by a group, frequently in quatrains, and ordinarily taking for its subject some kind of praise of God. Some still famous examples of hymns from the eighteenth-century Protestant tradition are: *When I Survey the Wondrous Cross* by Isaac Watts; *Hark! the Herald Angels Sing* by Charles Wesley; and *Rock of Ages* by a gentleman with the delightful name of Augustus Montague Toplady. These three names can be taken as symptomatic of the interest in hymns in the period, for Watts is early, Wesley middle, and Toplady late in the eighteenth century.

It must not be supposed, however, that the writing of hymns was exclusively the pursuit of such Dissenters, Methodists, and Calvinists as the persons named in the preceding paragraph. At the risk of pedantry, one might list a few other names partaking in the genre: Dryden, Addison, Parnell, Prior, Byrom, Gray, Smart, Thomson, Hannah More, Mrs. Barbauld, Chatterton, Cowper, Robert Newton, and Bowles. And the tones or attitudes of the hymn could be as numerous as the authors, ranging from the rather confident and staid Anglicanism of Addison to the somewhat depressed, incipient Calvinism of Cowper.

Although the hymn in the eighteenth century was written by many people of diverse backgrounds, it seems to have had a consistent tendency as far as its literary merits are concerned. For the great majority of the hymns of the period are simple, beautiful, unaffected, and remarkably unencumbered by overuses of the favorite diction of the day. Of course, not all of the hymnists directed their praise at the "right" object; Aikenside, for example, wrote a *Hymn to Science*, and Thomson composed a *Hymn on Solitude*. But generally the hymn is associated with the humbling of oneself before one's Maker.

The great activity in the genre in the eighteenth century is no doubt related to a large extent to religious and social history. It was an age in which several major Protestant movements were either founded or coming into their own; chief among these was Methodism, and of course every new idea needs its own poetry. Also the lower middle class, which since the politico-religious strife and the Glorious Revolution of the seventeenth century had been gaining power, wanted a literature more relevant to its needs and sensibilities—something a bit different from standard Anglicanism on the one hand and traditional heroic literature on the other. Here again the hymn was felt to be the appropriate vehicle.

But the rise of the hymn may not be *totally* tied up with religious and political history, for a good many hymns were produced by those who had no essential quarrel with either the Church or the social structure. It is possible that one reason the hymn found a number of writers is that it could be used as one more escape valve for lyricism, which was usually quashed by the doctrine of restraint. The reader is struck by Pope's shift to unrestrained emotional outpourings when the poet finds himself in the genre of the hymn:

> Vital spark of heavenly flame!
> Quit, oh quit this mortal frame:
> Trembling, hoping, lingering, flying,
> Oh the pain, the bliss of dying!

> Cease, fond nature, cease thy strife,
> And let me languish into life.

Though Pope entitles this *Ode: The Dying Christian to his Soul*, it is not merely the license of the ode that is at work here; for this is the very stuff of the hymn—simple, unaffected language in simple, easily singable lines.

Though the impulse toward lyricism may have had a large share in the furtherance of the hymn, it must be countered that to some degree the hymn is foreign to the lyric. Whereas the keynote of the lyric is personal expression, that of the hymn is *group* expression. It is significant in this respect that Pope generalizes in his title—"*The* Dying Christian"—making the poem widely applicable. Yet the hymn can serve the Augustan as a platform for intense displays of emotion. In a sense, the hymn is both lyrical and nonlyrical. Although it is intended for group use, it is usually written according to an impulse that, to the devout Christian, is intensely personal. In any case, whatever its motive, the eighteenth century has given succeeding periods some of the finest hymns in the language.

Sonnet

The sonnet is not a very important "kind" in eighteenth-century poetry, and the period produced relatively few such poems. That this genre was frowned upon or neglected in the period is shown not only by the scarcity of sonnets but also by the fact that perhaps as late as 1827 (the date of composition is unknown) Wordsworth felt it necessary to defend sonneteering. "Scorn not the sonnet," he wrote, for this was the type of poem in which "Shakespeare unlocked his heart" and which Milton used as a magnificent "trumpet." Actually, the great Romantic was overstating the case somewhat, for by the last quarter of the eighteenth century the sonnet had regained at least some of the respectability it had had in the Renaissance.

However, the new sonnet that emerged in the late Augustan period was somewhat different in temperament from its Renaissance counterpart. Whereas the great Elizabethans, with the exception of Milton, used the form almost exclusively to unlock their hearts on the subject of love (sacred or profane), the eighteenth-century sonnet is usually less interested in the personal, lyrical note and instead often focuses upon such matters as literature, philosophical concerns, and politics. For example, Thomas Edwards, one of the best sonneteers of the period, wrote sonnets defending Shakespeare and Milton, complimenting celebrities, giving advice to friends, singing the virtues of country retirement, praising patriotism, and urging the benefits of religion. Edwards flourished around the middle of the eighteenth century and influenced a group of minor or obscure figures including William Mason, Susannah Highmore, and John Duncombe. During the second half of the century, the production of sonnets increased to such a point that it was not unusual to see them appearing in groups—e.g., Thomas Warton's influential *Sonnets* (1777), Thomas Russell's *Sonnets and Miscellaneous Poems* (1789), and William Lisle Bowles's high quality *Sonnets* (also 1789). But generally it is safe to say that the period is not an age of sonnets.

Indeed, only a few decades ago it was the belief of modern scholarship that there were no extant sonnets from Milton to almost the middle of the eighteenth century. Scholarly human nature being what it is, this statement was taken as a challenge, and students of the period began digging to see if they could find traces of sonneteering activity in these blank years. Today scholarship knows of such rarities as a sonnet on love published by Philip Ayres in 1687, an anonymous political sonnet published in 1692, and another anonymous one on death published in 1735. More are turning up as time goes on, but no amount of scholarly sleuthing will make the eighteenth century any more fond of the sonnet than we know it to be at present.

For it seems that almost as frequently as it appeared the sonnet was attacked by the Augustans. A poem attributed to Samuel Johnson makes this charge:

> Yet, lay the sonnet for an hour aside,
> Its charms are fled and all its powers destroyed.

And as late as the last decade of the eighteenth century the sonnet was burlesqued by the appearance of a "pugilistical sonnet" and a "slang sonnet." No doubt a central reason for the unpopularity of the form was its traditional association with the personal note, which seemed to detract from the doctrine of writing about "what oft was thought," though this doctrine had become seriously undermined even before the middle of the century. Nevertheless, the conservatism against the sonnet lingered on and on, as can be seen by the somewhat paranoid overtones of Wordsworth, quoted at the beginning of this section. But one can say without bias that some of the opposition to the sonnet was justified. Even the best eighteenth-century poets were for some reason capable of writing incredibly bad sonnets; Gray's *Sonnet on the Death of Mr. Richard West* was justly deplored. Perhaps it was still too early for genuine and unstilted personal expression. Not until Bowles, who was very much respected by Coleridge, does the reader begin to sense strongly the old Renaissance lyrical impulse.

On the other hand, it would be an oversimplification to leave the impression that all Augustan sonnets were failures. Here, quoted in full, is the excellent *On a Family Picture* published in 1748 by Thomas Edwards, the best sonneteer before Bowles:

When pensive on that Portraiture I gaze,
Where my four brothers round about me stand,
And four fair sisters smile with graces bland,
The goodly monument of happier days;
And think how soon insatiate Death, who
        preys
On all, has cropped the rest with ruthless hand;
While only I survive of all that band,
Which one chaste bed did to my Father raise;
It seems that like a column left alone,
The tottering remnant of some splendid fane,
Scaped from the fury of the barbarous Gaul,
And wasting time, which has the rest
        o'erthrown;
Amidst our House's ruins I remain
Single, unpropped, and nodding to my fall.

Even a beginning reader will see the successful interweaving of imagery between octet and sestet. "The goodly monument" of line four prepares nicely for the ruins image in the sestet, and the image of "House" in line thirteen harks smoothly back to the concept of family in the octet. The rhythm is equally evocative, as in the extra syllable inserted into line ten through "tottering," the effect of which is to suggest the shuddering instability of the pillar about to topple over. And the final line, with its caesuras in the first part and unrestricted flow in the last part, helps the reader to sense the tentative swaying and then the headlong, irrevocable crashing down of the column. While it is true that the lines are for the most part end-stopped instead of run-on and flowing after the manner of Milton, Edwards's sonnet is still a very good poem in its own right.

It will be noticed that Edwards follows the traditional Italian or Miltonic format in dividing the thought into two units, a situation or problem in the octet and a response or solution in the sestet. This bipartite structure was by far the most popular among the eighteenth-century sonneteers. The Shakespearean structure, which consists of a thought-unit for each quatrain and a concluding couplet, was not to equal the Miltonic structure in popularity until the last decade of the century. Edwards is also symptomatic in his use of the Italian or Miltonic rhyme-scheme, *abbaabbacdecde*, for this was to be more popular in the period than the Shakespearean or English scheme of *ababcdcd efefgg*. And only very rarely did the century produce sonnets with the interlocking scheme of Spenser, *ababbcbccdcdee*.

Since the sonnet is chiefly a phenomenon of the late eighteenth century, it may seem irrelevant to think of it in terms of Augustan "rules." Yet there were several critics who at the end of the century tried to issue such dicta. For example, Anna Seward, "The Swan of Lichfield," declared that her own sonnets were written according to "rules deduced from the Miltonic sonnet," and that some of Milton's sonnets were the best possible "models"—just as an earlier Augustan might have said that Horace was the best model for the familiar epistle. Another late-eighteenth-century prescription came from Richard Polwhele, who maintained that the proper province of the sonnet was the "beautiful" (i.e., the pretty, the dainty, the orderly), not the "sublime" (i.e., the vast, the astonishing, the transporting—qualities associated with certain kinds of odes). Thus even in the late eighteenth century there was still enough of the old Augustan conservatism to spell out some "rules" for the "new" genre of the sonnet. On the other hand, a number of poets in the period, including the Swan of Lichfield herself, wrote poems of irregular rhyme-schemes and called them sonnets, just as Donne had entitled his collection *Songs and Sonnets* though no actual sonnet appeared in the collection. Donne, and perhaps the late-eighteenth century sonneteers too, may have had in mind the original Italian meaning of the term, "song" or "little sound." But some of the confusion was due to ignorance, for by the second half of the eighteenth century the sonnet had been neglected so long that as late as 1797 it was possible for the *Monthly Review* to declare in all innocence that Milton was "the first Englishman that was induced to attempt the sonnet in the language of our island"!

Ballad

In spite of its simple appearance, the ballad is so complicated and variable that no definition is going to do it justice. One may, however, suggest three tentative categories, all of which are relevant to the eighteenth century: traditional ballad, street ballad, and literary ballad.

The first definition fits many of the old ballads that, though composed centuries earlier, were popular and influential in the Augustan Age. This type of ballad frequently takes a love-tragedy as its subject; uses a sketchy, merely hinted-at plot; leans heavily upon scene and is thus somewhat dramatic; is objective in that the storyteller makes little or no effort to interpret the action; has a brief, rapid denouement; employs standard "ballad meter" (quatrains of alternating four-and three-stress lines in which only the second and fourth lines rhyme); and often uses a refrain, which may be incremental.

Two famous and powerful old ballads that have most of these characteristics are *Barbara Allen* and *Sir Patrick Spens*. (Incidentally, there was a time when such pieces were thought to be communal in origin, but later scholars feel that the social structure shown in them is too sophisticated to warrant such a conclusion. One thing is clear, however; this type of ballad was no doubt preserved and transmitted orally for a long time before being written down.) Ballads like *Barbara Allen* and *Sir Patrick Spens* are powerful, not for what they do, but for what they don't do. The precise nature of Barbara Allen's cruelty and revenge is never explained, nor is the motivation for Sir Patrick's voyage made exactly clear.

It may be just this somber and almost irrational mysteriousness, making the reader exercise his imagination, that accounts for the enduring popularity of such poems, not only in the Augustan Age but in the present century as well. Although this kind of ballad is by far the best, it was seldom produced in the eighteenth century, or indeed after the close of the Middle Ages in England. It was, however, enormously influential in the neoclassical period.

A second type of ballad relevant to the eighteenth century is the "broadside" or street ballad. Especially strong in the later seventeenth and earlier eighteenth centuries, the street ballad was usually composed in a hurry to commemorate or celebrate a major event; for example, a number of these appeared during and shortly after the great plague and fire of London in 1665–1666. But the street ballad was also used for political or economic events, as in Swift's *Upon the South-Sea Project.*

Already one can infer that the street ballad may be composed by any sort of writer, from the lowliest Grub Street hack to a major literary figure like Swift; and the range of artistry in these pieces is just as wide. *London Mourning in Ashes,* written to sing the London fire, ends with a moral:

> If this do not reform our lives,
> A worse thing will succeed,
> Our kindred, children, and our wives,
> Will dye for want of bread;
> When famine comes,
> 'Tis not our drums,
> Our ships, our horse or foot,
> That can defend,

> But if we mend,
> We shall never come to't.

This obvious piece of hack-work shows one of the many rhyme and stanza schemes used by the Augustan street ballad. Swift's *Upon the South-Sea Project* uses something a little closer to the traditional ballad meter:

> The nation then too late will find,
> Computing all their cost and trouble,
> Directors' promises but wind,
> South-sea at best a mighty bubble.

But it can easily be seen that both of the above examples moralize, and this at once separates them from the more objective, noncommital traditional ballad, such as *Sir Patrick Spens*. (Of course, the street ballad could occasionally be used for pure entertainment, as in Henry Carey's *Ballad of Sally in our Alley*, but such works are more *song* than ballad.)

Another respect in which the street ballad differs from the traditional ballad is that whereas the latter sets a certain emphasis upon storytelling or sketches of narratives, the former is not especially interested in plot. Rather, the street ballad as a rule focuses upon a central event or image for the purpose of making a particular point. And whereas the traditional ballad merely hints—often ominously—at an action, the street ballad customarily spells things out. Still another distinction between the two ballad types is that the street ballad is often a satirical weapon (it was frequently used in elections), whereas the traditional ballad generally has no element of attack outside of its own framework. But what is shared by the two types of ballad is a wide popular audience.

This last factor, a wide popular audience, may be used to help to define the third strain of balladry in the eighteenth century: the literary ballad. This type is extremely popular among *cultured readers* in the latter half of the eighteenth century. The central impetus in its development was the *Reliques*, collected by Thomas Percy, an amassing of a number of older English poems, including non-ballads, which appeared in 1765. (Percy's collection was anticipated by others, but it seems to have had by far the greatest influence upon the literary ballad). *Reliques* is strongly symptomatic of a new wave of interest in the traditional ballad, but that is not the book's real importance for the literary historian. What is interesting is the attempts in Percy's collection to "correct" or to "improve" the old ballads or to try to imitate them. The most notorious attempt at imitation was *Hardyknute*, which passed among many as a genuine relic; actually it was written by the contemporary Lady Wardlaw.

There were a number of forgeries like this, including the very good ones of Thomas Chatterton, but as time went on the emphasis tended to shift away from forgery to an honest attempt to recreate the atmosphere and the power of the traditional ballad. This is what finally gave rise to the literary ballad, the most famous example of which is, of course, Coleridge's *Ancient Mariner*, an effort of the modern poet to play the simple medieval bard.

But if one excepts the work of Chatterton and Coleridge, there is very little noteworthy poetry in this vein. Try as they might, the modern poets could not but be themselves. Even Chatterton's *Excelente Balade of Charity*, a good poem in its own right, is irredeemably Augustan in its stern didacticism, an element quite foreign to the traditional ballad ("We are God's stewards all, naught of our own we bear"). Similar troubles occur in Percy's rendering, *Friars of Orders Gray*, and in Goldsmith's *The Hermit*. Then again, too frequently the literary ballad is undone by its own "literariness," as can be seen in the stilted *Pastoral Ballad* of Shenstone:

> My banks they are furnished with bees,
> Whose murmur invites one to sleep,
> My grottos are shaded with trees,
> And my hills are white over with sheep.

Significantly, this piece was written before the middle of the century and shows that, even from the start, the Augustan was never going to project himself back into the true medieval mode.

It is not extravagant to say that for the most part the literary ballad was a failure as far as the eighteenth century was concerned; Johnson was justified in attacking such effusions. One could wish the period had stuck to its original tasks of producing rough but honest street ballads or reproducing for posterity the excellent traditional ballads.

In summary one might mention the fallacy in the view, popular not so many years ago, that only the later eighteenth century was sympathetic to the ballad. Actually the period was prolific in the genre from 1660 to 1800. It was said earlier that Percy's *Reliques* was an impetus for future ballad writing, but it can just as well be maintained that the collection was a manifestation of an already existing interest in the ballad. In any case, at no time in the period was the ballad a stranger to even the best of writers, as can be seen in Addison's warm praise of *Chevy Chase* (*Spectators* 70 and 74).

Anacreontic

The Anacreontic constitutes a small and not overwhelmingly important genre of Augustan poetry. Modeled after the Greek poet Anacreon (572?–448? B.C.), this type of poem is a short lyric that customarily takes women and wine for its two main subjects. It strives for a tone or atmosphere of grace and polish, and frequently achieves a high degree of artificiality (not necessarily a pejorative term in the eighteenth century). It is thought that the porcelain-like finish of Anacreon's poems (sometimes called odes) may have had to do with the gay court society in which the poet spent much of his life. In any case, the work of Anacreon is noted for its lack of "genuine" personal feeling. This, however, did not bother the Augustans, who for the most part were writing in an age when the lyric note had all but been pushed aside by the other genres and the doctrine of restraint.

The meter of Anacreon, consisting of three trochees and one "long" syllable at the end of the line, could not of course be exactly rendered into English. Thus the Augustans who tried to imitate the ancient poet had to concoct some other meter. Beattie, for example, tries to suggest the flavor of Anacreon through a kind of sing-song doggerel:

> Bathyllus, in yonder lone grove
> All carelessly let us recline:
> To shade us the branches above
> Their leaf-waving tendrils combine.

John Sheffield, Earl of Mulgrave, has better luck with a basic trochaic scheme upon which he works some beautiful variations:

> Thou flatterer of all the fair,
> Come with all your skill and care;
> Draw me such a shape and face,
> As your flattery would disgrace.
> Wish not that she would appear;
> 'Tis well for you she is not here.

But Parnell has some success with the regular iambic scheme:

> Gay Bacchus liking Estcourt's wine,
> A noble meal bespoke us;
> And for the guests that were to dine,
> Bright Comus, Love and Jocus.

And Prior varies from iambic to trochaic:

> Bid the warbling nine retire:
> Venus, string thy servant's lyre:
> Love shall be my endless theme:
> Pleasure shall triumph over Fame:
> And when these maxims I decline,
> Appollo, may thy fate be mine:
> May I grasp at empty praise;
> And lose the nymph, to gain the bays.

Like Parnell, Shenstone is satisfied with a regular iambic stanza pattern:

> 'Twas in a cool Aonian glade,
>   The wanton Cupid, spent with toil,
> Had sought refreshment from the shade;
>   And streched him on the mossy soil.

Samuel Johnson, with predictable regularity, maintains the same trochaic beat throughout his rendering in tetrameter couplets:

> Lovely courtier of the sky,
> Whence or whither dost thou fly?
> Scattering, as thy pinions play,
> Liquid fragrance all the way.

It is possible that Johnson's choice of meter was influenced by Ambrose Philips's version of *The Fourth Ode of Anacreon*:

> Hither loves and myrtles bring;
> Tender harvest of the spring:
> Soft and cool, my limbs recline;
> While I give myself to wine.

As can be seen from the above quotations, there was a problem as to how best to capture the flavor in English of the ancient poet. Incidentally, Philips was later to be criticized by Francis Fawkes, chief Augustan translator of Anacreon, for "mistaking the true sense" of the Greek writer ("Introduction" to *The Works of Anacreon*). That Fawkes could be relied upon as a good authority and imitator-translator of

Anacreon's poems is suggested by Johnson's remark that "Frank Fawkes has done them very finely" (*Thraliana*).

Though Anacreontics were not first introduced into English by the Augustans (Herrick had done a number of good ones), the genre seems to have attained its greatest popularity in the eighteenth century. If the Augustans could not quite bring themselves to compose unmitigated lyrics, they could at least approach the lyric through the avenue of the pretty artificiality of Anacreon. As the chronological span of authors quoted earlier may indicate, the Anacreontic had a long life in the eighteenth century.

Elegy

A book like this one, whose main focus is on specific genres and forms, is perhaps justified in giving little space to the elegy; for elegy is a kind of spirit or mood that can be found in any number of literary types. Elegy, as used in this discussion, means a tone or atmosphere of mourning (other meanings of elegy, or elegiac, are witty love poems after the manner of Ovid and Donne, or a specific classical meter). In English poetry a tone of mourning can be found practically anywhere, and this is especially true of the Augustan Age.

Elegy has always been associated with pastoral, and the eighteenth century follows suit by producing any number of pastoral elegies. Perhaps the best known is Gray's *Elegy Written in a Country Churchyard*, which, though not strictly a traditional pastoral, is pastoral nonetheless, having replaced the classical countryside with the fresh but saddened air of Stoke Poges, where Gray is supposed to have written his poem. Whenever important people died in eighteenth-century England, there were usually a number of poets to sing the deaths in more traditional pastoral elegies. One of the very best of these is the little-known (to the twentieth century) *Monody*, written by George, Lord Lyttelton, on his wife's death. But that elegy writing was sometimes overdone may be seen in Swift's statement that after his death the "Grub Street wits" will see to it that "With elegies the town is cloyed" *(Verses on the Death of Dr. Swift).*

Lyttelton's *Monody*, mentioned above, is every inch a pastoral elegy, but it also happens to be an ode written in what some Augustans construed as "Pindarics." The pastoral-elegiac-ode is not an especially rare bird in eighteenth-century poetry, nor is it unusual to find the spirit of elegy in other genres; Gay, for example, wrote a piece called *An Elegiac Epistle to a Friend.* One would not have to go far to find the spirit of elegy in the ballad, the hymn, the song, or any number of other Augustan kinds. Something as abstract as a tone or atmosphere can penetrate the walls of any genre. From the distant prospect of the twentieth century, the modern reader can see the wisdom of the Augustans in giving "few rules ... concerning the structure of elegiac poetry," as Shenstone said in his *Prefatory Essay on Elegy.*

IV

The Heroic and Exotic Veins

C hapter IV describes several of the genres or traditions through which the Augustans at-
tempted to move away from their customary concern with the actual and the immediate. Dealt with
here are the epic, the heroic epistle, the medieval or
Gothic tradition, the Oriental tradition, the doctrine
of the sublime, and the "school" of sensibility.

Epic

An epic is a long narrative poem dealing with
noble characters in a noble manner and arriving at
some overall unity, though it may be composed of a
number of episodes. Its action is on a large scale in
that it usually involves the fate of an entire nation, or
a race, or all mankind *(Paradise Lost)*. Other elements
frequently found in the epic are invocations of gods
or muses, interference in the action by the gods,
descriptions of armaments, councils of war, battles
on a grand scale, descents into the underworld, epic
similes, and a habit of beginning *in medias res* or "in

the middle of things." Some critics feel that epics can be written in prose (e.g., Sidney's *Arcadia* and Tolstoy's *War and Peace*).

The striking fact is that, although the eighteenth century revered the epic, not a single first-rate epic appeared in this neoclassical age. One can of course mention such not inept pieces as Cowley's *Davideis* and Davenant's *Gondibert*, but these works are unfinished and appear so early as to be almost outside of the Augustan period. The next decade saw the appearance of *Paradise Lost* (1667); but Milton's poem is by no means Augustan, and in any case, it is one of those masterpieces that have a way of transcending whatever milieu they are written in. One can point to Pope's Homer too, arguing that it is a loose enough translation to be a poem in its own right; but that is not the same as constructing an epic from the ground up. There are no successful true epics in the Augustan Age.

There were, however, several efforts that are of historical if not literary interest. Richard Blackmore had the energy to finish four epics: *Prince Arthur*, *King Arthur*, *Eliza*, and *Alfred*. The contemporary reception of these pieces may be suggested by the fact that the critic John Dennis was moved to write over two hundred pages attacking *Prince Arthur*. More than once Blackmore was accused of writing to the "rumbling of his coach's wheels." Another man brave or foolish enough to attempt a thoroughgoing epic was Richard Glover, who wrote the blank-verse *Leonidas*. Glover's epic made somewhat of a splash, but eighteenth-century readers found themselves loving or hating it according to their political biases, for the poem was unabashedly Whiggish. Just after mid-century, William Wilke produced *The Epigoniad* but failed to earn the title "the Scottish Homer." And a few years later James Macpherson brought forth one of the greatest literary hoaxes of all time, *Ossian*. There is some quality in Macpherson's work, just as there had been quality almost seventy years earlier in Samuel Wesley's *The Life of Our Blessed Lord*, inspired by *Paradise Lost*; but there was no truly great epic in the entire period.

It has been said that each national epoch has but one great epic in the storehouses of its intellect, but the facts indicate otherwise. In England alone the Renaissance saw at least two, *The Faerie Queene* and *Paradise Lost*, or three if one counts the *Arcadia*. Why the eighteenth century could not produce even one is a difficult question. One possible reason is that to have a great epic a nation must have a heroic image of man and of itself. If this is true, then by the eighteenth century it was too late, for this period marks the major shift from grand and traditional literature to writing that is more relevant to the modern, middle-class man. It is not by accident that the modern novel begins in the middle of the Augustan Age. In the epic genre, the very best that the period could furnish was the mock-epic brilliance of *The Rape of the Lock*.

Heroic Epistle

Whereas for at least two centuries the literary scene of Great Britain swarms with familiar epistles, the heroic epistle seems to receive scanty attention. Nevertheless, there are enough of these pieces to allow one to discern a faint genre and to draw some conclusions about it. A heroic epistle is an essentially nondramatic, versified letter addressed by a historical, legendary, or mythological persona of great or heroic stature to someone who is *usually* of such stature. It is often rendered in heroic couplets and customarily its subject is love. It may be of any length; but, like the familiar epistle, it ordinarily restricts itself to four hundred lines or less.

The chief classical model for the heroic epistle is Ovid, who produced two groups of poetic letters: the *Heroides* and the *Epistulae ex Ponto*. The *Heroides* are imaginary letters from famous ladies of legend or mythology to various heroes; some of the personae are Penelope, Medea, Phaedra, Dido, Ariadne, and Oenone. All of the great women of the *Heroides* share a common ailment, which is absence from a loved one, but each lady takes a different approach to her plight (e.g., Medea is remorseful, Phaedra passionate). Ovid's other group of letters, *Epistulae ex Ponto* or "Letters from the Black Sea," are written by the exiled poet in his own person, and are of more biographical than literary interest. The *Heroides* were the chief classical influence on the neoclassical heroic epistle.

There is very little Augustan criticism concerning the heroic epistle; indeed, one of the best statements occurs long before the eighteenth century, in the introduction to Michael Drayton's *England's Heroicall Epistles* (1619). This work was a collection of fictitious verse letters "written" by major figures of English history—for example, letters are exchanged by Richard II and his Queen Isabel, and by Henry II and Rosamond. Drayton gives the following explanation for his choice of the term "heroicall":

though heroical be properly understood of demi-
gods, as of Hercules and Aeneas, whose parents
were said to be, the one, celestial, the other, mortal; yet is it also transferred to them, who for the
greatness of mind come near to gods. For to be
born of a celestial incubus, is nothing else, but to
have a great and mighty spirit, far above the
earthly weakness of men; in which sense Ovid
(whose imitator I partly profess to be) doth also
use heroical.

Thus the practice of using real persons from recent
history was established by Drayton, who anticipates
the eighteenth century not only in his subject matter
but also in his heroic couplet style. It is not surprising that Drayton was admired by many Augustans.

One other valuable criticism needs to be mentioned. *Spectator* 618, which discusses the familiar
epistle, also contains some thoughts on the heroic,
though that specific term is not used. Of the proper
Ovidian (heroic) epistle, the writer declares that

he that is ambitious in succeeding in the Ovidian
way, should first examine his heart well, and
feel whether his passions (especially those of the
gentler kind) play easy, since it is not his wit,
but the delicacy and tenderness of his sentiments, that will affect his readers. His versification likewise should be soft, and all his numbers
flowing and querulous.

According to the implications of this dictum, then, it
is the particular business of the heroic epistle to deal
with love, as is the practice of Ovid and Drayton; and

love of one kind or another is the major subject matter of the heroic epistles produced by the eighteenth
century.

Love, religious and sexual, is the topic of the
finest heroic epistle of the age, Pope's *Eloisa to
Abelard,* as it is in James Cawthorn's imitation
Abelard to Eloisa. Frivolous, promiscuous love is the
chief ingredient of *A Very Heroical Epistle in Answer
to Ephelia* by John Wilmot, Earl of Rochester, the
Restoration rake, who argues to Ephelia that the best
love is that experienced by a sultan who controls a
very large harem. It scarcely needs pointing out that
Rochester's use of the word "heroical" is facetious—a
manifestation of the Augustan tendency simultaneously to exploit and satirize the genres. Manly,
friend-to-friend love is the essence of John Byrom's
*A Poetical Version of a Letter, from the Earl of Essex to
the Earl of Southhampton* and of Ann Finch's *Epistle
from Alexander to Hephaestion.* The disappointment
of heroic love is the topic of William Whitehead's
Ann Boleyn to Henry the Eighth and of *Helen to Paris,*
an imitation of Ovid by John Sheffield, Earl of
Mulgrave. A better Ovidian imitation is Elijah Fen-
ton's *Phaon to Sappho.* Swift, in his customary per-
verse way, wrote a sneering heroic epistle called
Apollo to the Dean, in which the god protests the
lack of adoration shown him by mortal men.

Later in the Augustan period, Mrs. Barbauld produced *Ovid to his Wife,* a poem that she claims is "imitated from different parts of Ovid's *Tristia.*" Robert
Burns wrote a *Lament of Mary Queen of Scots* which,
although it is not labeled a heroic epistle, still
belongs in the genre, due to the heroic stature of the
persona and to the fact that she addresses Queen

Elizabeth and the future King James I. Another later eighteenth-century writer worth noticing is Hannah More, whose *Heroic Epistle to Sally Horne,* addressed to a three-year-old and focused on morality for children, suggests that by this time the genre was rapidly losing whatever specific identity it had had in the first place. Yet there is enough of this elevated epistolary verse to enable one to see an identifiable tradition of the heroic epistle throughout most of the Augustan Age.

Regarding style and organization, one may readily take his clue from the pronouncements of *Spectator* 618, quoted above. The style should be "flowing and querulous"; that is, the heroic epistle's language, though elevated, tends to avoid the close syntax and tight compression ordinarily associated with the heroic couplet. Such rigid architecture seems foreign to the sentiment of love. It is interesting to note that whenever Pope's Eloisa falls into the style of, say, *Essay on Criticism* or *Essay on Man,* the result is an invariable gaucherie:

> I view my crime, but kindle at the view,
> Repent of pleasures, and solicit new;
> Now turned to Heaven, I weep my past offence,
> Now think of thee, and curse my innocence.

Such rigorous parallelism, antithesis, and conscious placing of caesuras goes against the "flowing and querulous" sentiment of love. It is better when Pope imitates the natural speech of distressed love: "I have not yet forgot myself to stone."

In organization, the heroic epistle exhibits much of the casualness found in the familiar epistle. But there is an important difference; for whereas the familiar epistle moves from a kind of rambling disorder to an orderly and positive assertion of a thesis, the heroic tends to maintain the casualness throughout, as if to suggest that there can be no thesis in love because it is a matter of emotion rather than of thought.

One might conclude a consideration of the heroic epistle in the eighteenth century with the reflection that such a genre can be seen as still another way in which the poet can practice lyricism under the doctrine of restraint.

Medieval or Gothic Tradition

The somewhat nostalgic use of medieval themes or material is never really absent from English literature; and although the great flowering of pseudo-medievalism is properly placed in the second half of the eighteenth century, it is thoroughly anticipated by the earlier Augustans. Moreover, the Augustans are anticipated by the Renaissance, as in the hermits and castles of the *Faerie Queene*. There is no such thing as an era in English literature that totally ignores the Gothic. The only period that comes very close to being a vacuum is the Restoration; but even here the major figure, Dryden, could compose his opera *King Arthur*, praise Chaucer in his *Preface to the Fables*, and seriously consider writing an epic about Edward the Black Prince.

In the early Augustan period there was of course much lip service to the effect that the Middle Ages were rude and barbarous times, hardly worthy of the attention of the cultivated Londoner. Yet at the same time Pope seized upon the Gothic framework of *Eloisa to Abelard* and loaded it with Gothic imagery. Eloisa refers to

> These moss-grown domes with spiry
> turrets crowned,
> Where awful arches make a noonday night,

and she mentions the "dreary wastes,"

> Where round some mouldering tower pale
> ivy creeps,
> And low-browed rocks hang mouldering
> o'er the deeps.

There is little difference between this imagery and the sort of pictures to be painted by the Gothic novelist Ann Radcliffe many years later.

Several years before Pope's poem, Addison had sung the praises of the medieval matter of *Chevy Chase* (*Spectator 70*), though he had Johnson's and Sidney's precedents, and took the precaution to make sure the old ballad could be measured by neoclassical rules. But what is important is that Addison *liked* the medieval matter. And a dozen years later, Mallet was to try to pass off the beautiful *William and Margaret* as his own, not wishing to be original like Parnell, who a few years before had produced his own "ballad," *The Hermit*. The Graveyard School too was part of the urge to affect the medieval. Though somewhat submerged, the love of the Gothic is very much alive in the first half of the century.

It is around mid-century that some literary

historians place the beginning of the great Gothic revival. As suggested above, there was no actual "revival," but there certainly was at this point an intensification of activity, chiefly in the work of Gray, Collins, and the Wartons. These poets frequently used specifically Gothic matter for whole poems (as in Gray's *The Bard*) or worked in large amounts of incidental medievalism (as in Collins's *Ode, Written in the Beginning of the Year, 1746*, more commonly known as "How Sleep the Brave"). After the appearance of Macpherson's Ossianic poems and Percy's *Reliques*, both in the 1760s, writers became less furtive about exploiting the medieval mode. Succeeding years saw so many imitations and forgeries that, by the time of the great Romantics, it seemed rather natural for such major figures as Coleridge and Keats to select the medieval tradition for some of their best work. One late-eighteenth-century "pre-Romantic" deserving special mention is Chatterton, who with his Rowley poems had everyone fooled until Walpole sent them to the scholarly Gray who immediately pronounced them forgeries. But they were good poetry in their own right.

This discussion has deliberately avoided a close definition of *Gothic* because like elegy or Orientalism, Gothic is much more of a general spirit than a specific genre. It is a temper of writing that creeps into any number of types—everything from the ballad and ode to the "terror" novels of Radcliffe and Lewis. Throughout most of the eighteenth century the term *Gothic* was so vast in its scope of meaning as to include anything from Old Norse mythology to the Renaissance. Its connotation was variable too; for it could suggest any quality from the rude and barbarous to the sublime, though as the century went on it tended to shift from pejorative to laudatory. Another factor working against precise definitions of Gothicism is that it is inextricably tied up with the broad tradition of melancholy, popular and widespread in English literature since before the Renaissance.

One can, however, suggest reasons for the fad of pseudo-medievalism that bulked so large in the last half of the century. For one thing, it offered an escape from the present, the here and now, which had for so long dominated the poetry. Whereas the "pre-Romantic" fashion of Orientalism (discussed in the next section) was a movement away in space, Gothicism was a movement away in time. And both movements showed a love of the wild and the unrestrained, which was to be a keynote for the great Romantics. In short, the love of the medieval was largely a way to get out from under the doctrine of restraint. But even in the early eighteenth century, when the doctrine of restraint was predominant, the movement was already afoot.

Another reason for the Gothic interest was that the concept of nature was changing throughout the century. Starting at least as early as the 1740s, there were many intellectuals who no longer saw nature as regular, symmetrical, and Newtonian; it was no longer "methodized" but rather had become as unrestrained as a cataract. The Gothicist could argue, with the Orientalist, that he was merely following nature.

Still another possible reason for the Gothic fashion was that people's view of themselves had undergone a change. By mid-century, many thinkers no longer gave much credit to the idea that the history of culture had been one of progressive decadence since the classical Golden Age or the analogous Biblical Fall of Man. If the Golden Age idea was a fallacy, then the medieval period could be seen as a furthering of culture, not a ruining of it. It is tempting to say that the Middle Ages had been reinstated, but this is not entirely the case. For what the Gothicists were writing about was their *image* of medieval times, not medieval times themselves—just as earlier poets had written about their *version* of classical times and not the real thing.

Of course, not everyone in the late eighteenth century was receptive to the Gothic strain; there were numerous parodies and burlesques, not to mention outright hostilities. One of the best pieces of satire on the pseudo-medievalist is Johnson's *Parody of Thomas Warton:*

> Hermit hoar, in solemn cell,
> Wearing out life's evening gray;
> Smite thy bosom, sage, and tell,
> Where is bliss? and which the way?
>
> Thus I spoke; and speaking sighed;
> Scarce repressed the starting tear;—
> When the smiling sage replied—
> —Come, my lad, and drink some beer.

This is good medicine for an ailment that one too frequently finds in the Gothicists—and in the Romantics—they take themselves too seriously. Nevertheless, the medieval strain produced some good poetry.

Oriental Tradition

Orientalism, which is more of a general influence than a specific genre, is the use in English culture of designs, images, narratives, or attitudes supposedly derived from the East; that is, the East in its broadest sense—Asia, the Near East, and Africa.

Poets are often thought to be prophets who anticipate by many years the directions that cultures will take. In Augustan England, however, it was not this way at all; for if one excepts the pseudo-Oriental matter of Renaissance and Restoration tragedies, the first real fascination with the East appears in the more mundane areas of interior design and landscaping. Long before the close of the seventeenth century, there was a fascination with "Sharawadgi" (a word supposedly derived from Chinese), a type of design that accented the wild, the surprising, the irregular. Sir William Temple helped to lend prestige to "Sharawadgi" by praising Oriental culture (*Essay upon Heroick Virtue*), and before another generation had passed, the East was gaining a foothold in literature.

At first, however, the East made itself felt only in the prose, as in Addison's *Vision of Mirzah* (*Spectator* 159). Addison's repeated use of the Oriental matter in his *Spectator* lent enough respectability to the tradition to influence later prose writers: Lord Lyttelton published his *Persian Letters*; Johnson produced his *Rasselas* and shorter Oriental pieces in the *Rambler*; Goldsmith wrote *The Citizen of the World*; and William Beckford brought forth his strange *Vathek*. In the meantime, translations of the *Arabian Nights* had become favorite reading, and later in the century translations of Voltaire's *Zadig* were popular.

The Oriental tradition in eighteenth-century English literature is chiefly a matter of prose. When one turns to the poetry, one learns that the first major event does not occur until 1742, the date of Collins's *Persian Eclogues*. Perhaps because it tries to move away from the immediate and the "civilized," the eclogue or pastoral found itself eminently suited for Oriental matter. In any case, Collins's work was followed by (to name only the more successful pastoral efforts) *Solima, an Arabian Eclogue* by Sir William Jones; *African Eclogues* by Chatterton; *Eastern Eclogues* by Eyles Irwin; and *Oriental Eclogues* by John Scott. Of course, the East did make its way into other types of poetry—Blake's *Little Black Boy*; Burns's facetious epitaph on "Queen Artemisa"; Churchill's *The Farewell*; Cowper's bitter *Pity for Poor Africans*; and John Langhorne's *Fables of Flora: Fable VI: The Queen of the Meadow and the Crown Imperial*. From the several genres represented by the poems mentioned in this paragraph, it can be seen that the Oriental tradition, like that of the elegy, was fluid enough to seep into a number of different poetic kinds. By the time of the major Romantics, it was in and through all of poetry.

The poems mentioned above may serve to demonstrate one other trait of Orientalism—it could be used for a variety of purposes. For the poems run the gamut from lyricism (Blake) to caustic satire (Cowper) to escapism (Collins) to ordinary humor (Burns). Such was the flexible nature of Eastern culture as interpreted by the eighteenth-century poet.

Though not overwhelmingly important as art, the eighteenth-century Oriental tradition is significant in the history of culture and ideas. As mentioned earlier, "Sharawadgi" implied wildness and irregular design; as such it could serve as a means for undermining the order and regularity of the neoclassical. Without stating that poetic Orientalists existed solely for the purpose of ushering in Romanticism, one can say that the effusions of the East definitely anticipate the love of the wild and the irregular that one finds in the great Romantics. Also to be noted is the way Orientalism parallels Gothicism: both accent lack of restraint, and both are movements away from the actual and the immediate—the Gothic in time, the Oriental in space. On the other hand, it should be added that all too often the Persian shepherds or Eastern sultans are really Englishmen in costume, just as Shakespeare's many Italians are actually Londoners. What mattered was the Englishman's *version* of the East, not the East itself. What matters even more is good poetry, not veracity of statement or of description.

The Sublime

The word *sublime* refers to a powerful quality in literature or nature. Though there are no exact synonyms for the word, some near misses might be: vast, astonishing, transporting, lofty, noble, terrifying (in a pleasurable way), grand, solemn, awe-inspiring, profoundly moving, haughty, proud, elevating, and (to use modern slang) absolutely mind-blowing.

Like many other traditions in the eighteenth century, the sublime as a doctrine began in classical times, in a document attributed to Longinus, a Greek rhetorician and philosopher who lived in the third century A.D. The influence of Longinus in England began in the late seventeenth century, and the popularity of the sublime reached its high point about the middle of the 1700s, after which it declined. For Longinus himself, the sublime was a matter of style and rhetoric; for the earlier Augustans, it was a matter of thought; for the mid-eighteenth-century and later writers, it was a matter of feeling or passion.

The counterpart of the sublime was the beautiful. The beautiful was held to be neat, orderly, pretty, exact, quiet, and down-to-earth, rather than lofty or transporting. It is no overstatement to say that the Augustans, especially the later ones, were overwhelmingly more interested in the sublime than in the beautiful. They abandoned the "beautiful" manicured gardens with their symmetrical walkways to seek the sublime in shattered ruins or wild natural scenery. Thomas Gray found it in the Alps and wrote home to his mother about it:

It is six miles to the top; the road runs winding up to it, commonly not six feet broad; on one hand is the rock, with woods of pine-trees hanging over head; on the other, a monstrous precipice, almost perpendicular, at the bottom of which rolls a torrent, that sometimes tumbling along the fragments of stone that have fallen from on high, and sometimes precipitating itself down vast descents with a noise like thunder, which is still made greater by the echo from the mountains on each side, concurs to form one of the most solemn, the most romantic, and the most astonishing scenes I ever beheld.

It is not hard to pick out the jargon of the sublime in Gray's language; however, it could be argued that the poet half-created what he saw. Long before he encountered the alpine scene, the doctrine of the sublime had conditioned him to respond in a certain way. The same scene to Shakespeare and his contemporaries would probably have appeared ugly and monstrous, the result of Adam's original sin, when not only man but also nature fell.

From time to time critics have suggested that the doctrine of the sublime was instrumental in breaking down the restrictions and rigidities of neoclassicism. But the truth seems to be that rather than do away with neoclassical rules, the sublime merely replaced them with a new set of laws. In any case, there is a kind of sameness in the "sublime" poets of the mid- and later-eighteenth century, as though they all wrote to the same prescription. The reader senses this sameness in the vocabularies of the *Winter* section of Thomson's *Seasons*, Collins's *Ode to Fear*, Gray's *The Bard*, and a number of less successful pieces by less important writers.

It is an irony of literary history that the mid-and late-eighteenth century, a period that loved the sublime, was able to produce so little poetry that really is sublime. Unfortunately this period is a kind of backwater, or eddying place, in the stream of English literature, competent though undistinguished for the most part. But although very little sublime poetry was produced, the doctrine of the sublime is still worthy of study as a major cultural phenomenon.

Sensibility

If the epic and the heroic represent flights upward, and if the Gothic and the Oriental are removals in time and space respectively, then the concept of "sensibility," so popular in the later eighteenth century, can be said to be a retreat into the inner man. Though it is more important in prose and drama than in poetry, it is dealt with here because no late-eighteenth-century poet completely escaped it. Although it is probably strongest in the "graveyard school," it makes its presence felt in such later topographical poems as Goldsmith's *Deserted Village*, and it can be sensed in many of the "lyrics" of the later Augustans.

Any discussion of sensibility would do well to offer a preliminary *caveat*. All attempts to define the term must fail, if only because it has been applied indiscriminately to practically everything in the later eighteenth century. What follows, then, is an existential effort to suggest some items that might be subsumed under the heading of eighteenth-century sensibility. It is sometimes useful to think of sensibility as a kind of Romanticism manqué.

An overriding attitude of sensibility is that the feelings, not the reason, should be the guide to truth. Beyond this, we may note the sentiments of several important writers on the subject. Suggesting that the germ of the idea is already there in the middle of the seventeenth century, Benjamin Whichcote declared that "all vice is unnatural"—a sentiment central to the major sensibility thesis that man is naturally good if only given a chance. Early in the 1700s, the Third Earl of Shaftesbury felt that we should "be persuaded that wisdom is more from the *heart* than from the *head.*" A little later, the philosopher David Hume wrote that "morality is more properly felt than judged of." And he was echoed by Rousseau, who argued that "the acts of conscience are not judgements, but sentiments." At the end of the period, Madame de Staël put it even more succinctly when she said that virtue is a "spontaneous impulsion."

A list of the ingredients of sensibility might include the following items. There is an accent on simplicity, which often manifests itself in a setting of rural solitude. There is also a strong faith in, and optimism toward, humanity—quite different from the more jaundiced views of satirists earlier in the century. Moreover, there is a heavy stress on nature in the sense of (1) external, physical nature and (2) the uncitified or unpolished. A fourth ingredient is a love of charity and a general feeling of benevolence toward one's fellow man. As might be inferred from such benevolence, sensibility rather automatically adopts a thesis that the social hierarchy should be flattened or at least foreshortened somewhat to reduce the "shameful variance betwixt man and man" (quoted from Thomson's *Seasons: Winter,* which is a fairly consistent sensibility poem of the early 1700s). A fifth ingredient is an emphasis on the intimate and the personal; sixth is a sometimes maudlin sentimentality—when sensibility is at its worst. This begets the seventh ingredient, the melodramatic. And closely related to the melodramatic is the eighth part, a frequent accent on fear and terror; this is one of several points at which the sublime and the school of sensibility intersect. Another ingredient of sensibility can be stated in

terms of certain type-characters who appear again
and again in this literature; two popular ones are the
fainting female and the sensitive, emaciated youth
who has retired from the world. It is not surprising to
learn that, in the fiction of this period, consumption
is a fashionable way to die. Sensibility plays a large
part in the Gothic, and one critic has suggested that
the Gothic arises from "a dissociation of conscience
from sentiment." That is, the kind of pseudo-
medieval excitement that one associates with such
novelists as Ann Radcliffe or Horace Walpole is predicated on sheer feeling devoid of the moral sense,
whereas true sensibility is a sort of *felt morality*.
Finally, as an ingredient of sensibility, one might
mention the obvious delight that such writers take in
melancholy. There is probably no such thing as a
period in English literature when pleasurable
melancholy is not popular or fashionable; but it is
especially strong in the late eighteenth century,
when the school of sensibility is in full session.

The process of assessing the value of sensibility
literature is made easy by the fact that, when fur-
nishing examples of this kind of writing, one has to
resort frequently to minor figures or works: Henry
Mackenzie's *The Man of Feeling* for the novel,
Richard Cumberland's *The Brothers* for the drama,
and a few less-than-major writers for the poetry. On
the other hand, it is worth noting that major figures
(e.g., Wordsworth or Jane Austen) either closely controlled sensibility or thumbed their noses at it.

V

Satire

Though it is the practice of this book to refrain, for the sake of simplicity, from mentioning modern critics in the text, the complexity of satire and of the modern criticism surrounding it calls for a temporary change of pattern. This chapter will begin with a survey of some important modern theories of, and comments on, satire and then move to a consideration of Augustan theories. After that, the discussion will deal with the history, manifestations, and implications of eighteenth-century satire.

Northrop Frye in his *Anatomy of Criticism* says that before we can call a work satire, it must have (1) wit or humor and (2) attack. Frye envisions a kind of spectrum, within which satire is defined; one of the boundaries is pure wit or humor without attack, the other pure attack without humor. Frye also allows that satire is not so much a strict genre as it is a "tone or attitude."

Like most of Frye's criticism, this is a very sane approach to things; but we should argue with the establishing of humor as a permanent characteristic of satire. The Juvenalian tradition, especially, is marked, from Juvenal himself to Johnson's great imitations, by a singular lack of humor. That is, though occasionally there may occur a brief passage of heavy-handed irony or wit in the piece, such humor is only incidental and thus cannot very well be said to be a defining characteristic of satire. And surely one is going to be hesitant to dismiss the whole of the Juvenalian tradition from the category of satire.

Another interesting part of Frye's theory of satire is his division of it into three levels or phases. On the first level, the satirist is generally satisfied with the social structure, even though he knows it isn't perfect, as in the *Satires* and *Epistles* of Horace. In the second phase, the satirist is dissatisfied with his society and wishes to replace it; that is, he objects to the existing social structure but still believes that *some* kind of social structure can work. The third level is the nihilistic one, for here the satirist not only is dissatisfied with his society but also feels that *no* social structure will work. Juvenal is a good example of the second phase, Orwell of the third.

A second modern critic intelligent and brave enough to venture a definition of satire is Maynard Mack, in his "Muse of Satire" (*Yale Review*, XLI, 1951). Like Frye, he constructs a spectrum, but this time tragedy and satire are the extremes. Satire, according to Mack, "asserts the validity and necessity of norms," whereas tragedy "tends to exhibit the inadequacy of norms."

We are immediately confronted with a dilemma, for it is possible that tragedy, like satire, *does* assert the validity of norms. If we accept, even metaphorically, a possible "tragic flaw" in the traditional

tragic hero, we can argue that Macbeth, who was ambitious, that Hamlet, who was indecisive, and that
Oedipus, who was rash, are all vivid examples of
deviations from the ideal norm. Consequently these
plays are tacitly, if not explicitly, suggesting that
there is an overwhelming necessity for norms.
Though the above examples are simplified, it is still a
valid point that satire and tragedy can just as well be
closely related as be opposites.

Another significant part of Mack's essay is his
contention that the "Muse of Satire" is merely a persona or dramatic speaker, and not necessarily the
satirist himself; that is, the voice speaking in the
satire may not be that of the author. Such a dramatic
speaker may uphold the norm or oppose it, while the
author himself may be somewhere in between the
ideal norm and the deviation from it.

Mack's theory is based on the belief that there *is*
such a thing as a persona, but a number of recent
critics feel that any voice in a literary work is always
that of the author and that there is no such thing as a
dramatic speaker—even the fiend advocating can-
nibalism in *A Modest Proposal* is a genuine facet of
Swift's personality. Some feel that the whole argument about personae is a quibble in terms. Probably
the best thing about a belief in a persona is that it
enriches one's literary experience. The worst thing
about it is that it can too easily be used to whitewash
writers and facilely excuse them from defects of
character, ethics, and philosophy that they may actually have.

Another critic who sees a relationship between
tragedy and satire is Philip Pinkus, in his "Satire and
Saint George" (*Queen's Quarterly*, Spring, 1963). Ac-

cording to Pinkus, evil dominates in satire, so that not Saint George but the Dragon wins. Thus the satirist is a kind of existential hero who derives his dignity through his struggle and refusal to give up, rather than through any kind of triumph over evil. The difference between tragedy and satire, then, is that the tragic hero triumphs *in spite* of evil while the satirist triumphs *because* of evil.

An important definition of satire occurs in Alvin Kernan's *The Cankered Muse*, which, though it is more relevant to the Renaissance, is still quite useful to the student of the eighteenth century. Kernan's scheme consists of three parts: "scene," "satirist," and "plot."

The scene in satire is crowded, disorderly, and smacking of rottenness; yet somewhere in this chaos there is a hint of the ideal that the satirist wishes to uphold.

The satirist, according to Kernan, has two personalities, the public and the private. The first is that of a plain-spoken, honest person of rather humble origins, who, though normally calm and controlled, is moved to indignation by the decadence of society. The private personality is quite another matter, for lurking behind the public image is a seamier individual who actually seems to revel in the nastiness of the scene he has created and to enjoy being just as mean and irrational as whatever it is that he's attacking.

Plot, the third ingredient in satire, is a kind of anti-plot, in the sense that the work has not a definite plot development but rather a sense of "constant movement without change." That is, the unpleasantness with which the satire began is merely intensified, not done away with or transformed into some kind of goodness as at the end of a comedy. This lack of progress contributes to what Kernan calls the "tone of pessimism in the genre."

Though Kernan offers a useful and provocative definition, many readers would quarrel with his point about "pessimism in the genre." In the first place, satire is more of a spirit or temper of writing than a specific genre. Secondly, to state that satire has "a tone of pessimism" ignores a fundamental conscious motivation in the writing of practically all pre-twentieth-century satire: faith in humanity. There are, it is true, certain striking exceptions—perhaps Book IV of *Gulliver's Travels*—but the average Augustan satirist, though he may not have blindly believed in "progress," did believe in man. The satirists of past ages are not likely to have wasted their ink upon something totally incorrigible, even while admitting that large parts of their works were written merely to entertain.

Still another definition of satire appears in the introduction of Edward W. Rosenheim's *Swift and the Satirist's Art*, which states that "satire consists of an attack by means of a manifest fiction upon discernible historical particulars." This is another spectrum, which places satire between the extremes of fact and fiction:

...ure Fiction	*Satire*	*Pure Fact*
omedy or hilosophic Myth	Persuasive Punitive	Rhetoric

From the chart it can be seen that comedy or philosophic myth lies in the realm of fiction, whereas rhetoric deals with fact and real life. Satire puts the two together, using a fiction (e.g., a country of miniature people) to attack a real or historical situation (e.g., the adminstration of Sir Robert Walpole in the first half of the eighteenth century). The result of these parenthetical examples is the satire in the first book of *Gulliver's Travels*.

Rosenheim employs the term *persuasive* to designate the kind of satire that is actually trying to convert people or change their attitudes; this kind of satire is closely allied to rhetoric. *Punitive* satire is the type that entertains its readers at the target's expense, without attempting to change anyone's opinion; this type is closely allied to comic or serious fiction.

Rosenheim's ingenious theory is more beautiful than applicable. This shortcoming is demonstrated in the later sections of his book in which he tries to apply his ideas to the writings of Swift. The *Argument Against the Abolishing of Christianity*, for example, is a satire of persuasion using for its facts or "historical particulars" the attitude of the nominal Christian, which, Rosenheim insists, was a very real attitude in the earlier eighteenth century. But if something so abstract and general as a mere attitude can be said to be a historical particular, so can practically anything. There is also the problem that rhetoric, at least as traditionally conceived, leans rather heavily upon fiction for its narratives, exempla, or other illustrations. On the other hand, *The Battle of the Books* is held by Rosenheim to be practically all punitive satire, and thus close to comedy.

But Rosenheim seems to soft-pedal the truth that the quarrel between ancients and moderns is a historical fact. He also overlooks the possibility that even "pure" comedy, as sure as it contains conflict, is automatically attacking or devaluating something or someone.

In short, the chief difficulty with Rosenheim's theory is that, like many theories, it breaks down in the definition of terms. What, finally, *are* fiction, fact, rhetoric, comedy, myth, etc.? A thorough analysis of all such terms would have to take place before a theory using them could get off the ground.

Yet the above theories of Frye, Mack, Pinkus, Kernan, and Rosenheim exhibit brilliance and are certainly provocative. And it is worth remembering that one of the major purposes of criticism is not so much to be "right" as to provoke valuable thought. The above-named scholars succeed admirably in this.

To this point, the discussion has centered more on definitions than on comments. The following survey deals with some critics who, while not trying actually to define satire, contribute useful observations.

Though he later softened his remarks, T. S. Eliot wrote in 1930 that the "satirist is in theory a stern moralist castigating the vices of his time or place" (*Poetry in the Eighteenth Century*, which originally appeared as an introduction to Johnson's imitations of Juvenal). Thus Eliot was able to declare that the satirical writings of Samuel Johnson, because of their seriousness of approach and target, are "purer" satires than those of Dryden and Pope, who theoretically are less stern, less castigating, and less concerned with vice. The trouble with Eliot's view is that it excludes the lighter kind of satire, which, though less serious, is satire nonetheless. Eliot comes close to saying that the Juvenalian tradition is real satire and the Horatian is not. Such a judgment seems arbitrary, though Eliot's remark is useful as an accurate delineation of the Juvenalian tradition in England in the eighteenth century.

Better comments occur in Ian Jack's *Augustan Satire*. Though the book is primarily concerned with the various modes of mock-heroic and with levels of diction, Jack makes one point that is extremely important in any general discussion of satire. This is his concept of the *ripple*; that is, satires, while they may focus chiefly on one main target, can make side-attacks on other targets. For example, *Hudibras* selects as its main target the Roundheads, but at the same time glances at bad taste in literature. Similarly, *The Rape of the Lock*, while it is assailing the frivolities of the *beau monde*, glances at injustice ("And wretches hang that jury men may dine").

Jack's concept of the ripple touches on a general truism about satire—that it is centrifugal in nature. As Robert C. Elliott points out in his *The Power of Satire*, an attack on a local phenomenon (e.g., dishonest priests) may easily expand itself into an attack on the whole structure of which that local phenomenon is a part (e.g., God and the Church). Satire always seems to work outward, starting perhaps with an isolated individual but ending up with the individual turned into a type-character common in the general experience of mankind.

Other useful comments appear in James Sutherland's *English Satire*. Sutherland maintains that comedy is not satire because, even though the writer of comedy may have opinions about moral standards, his chief aim is something other than the upholding of these standards, something other than lashing vice and folly. The comedy writer is detached, whereas the satirist, at least in regard to his public image, is very much involved in the moral struggle. Sutherland is one of the few modern critics who hold a thoroughly moral view of satire; the satirist writes, according to this critic, because "he thinks nobly of the human soul."

Another valuable comment was furnished to the present writer by one of his former professors, Donald Cornu of the University of Washington. His statement is that a satirical work can be assessed in terms of *amperage* and *voltage*. Amperage refers to the artistry and subtlety of the piece, voltage to the importance of the target. Thus many of the beautifully written items in such magazines as *The New Yorker* or *Punch*, if they were directed at trivialities like poor table manners, would be classified as high amperage and low voltage. In eighteenth-century literature, no one is likely to question the proposition that *Gulliver* is high amperage *and* high voltage; or that *The Rape of the Lock* is for the most part high amperage and *low* voltage. Two other possibilities remain: low amperage and high voltage, and low amperage *and* low voltage. For examples of both the reader is referred to his local newspaper.

Two early-twentieth-century thinkers who have shed much light on the action and imagery of satire are Freud and Bergson. In his *Jokes and Their Relation to the Unconscious*, Freud advances his theory about "economy of expenditure." He says that one reason we laugh at others is that they do things the hard way. As we watch a small child trying to screw a lid on a jar and having a hard time of it, we make a preconscious comparison between the child's over-use of energy and our own presumably more efficient way of getting the job done. To ourselves, we are masters of the economy of expenditure. A moment's reflection will show that the characters who are the objects of satire very frequently do simple things with great difficulty. Belinda in *The Rape of the Lock* needs enormous amounts of space, time, help, and paraphernalia to get her make-up on; and the whole poem, with its "needless" application of heavy epic machinery to a very slight narrative, is a sustained instance of Freud's principle.

Bergson's famous essay, *Laughter*, advances the theory that the comic arises from "something mechanical encrusted on the living." That is, whenever life, which is fluid, flexible, and ever-changing, is forced into a rigid pattern, it becomes potentially funny. Whenever human beings and human situations begin to resemble machines, they are moving toward the ludicrous. A simple example would be Major Hoople of *Our Boarding House* in the newspaper comics, who, regardless of the situation, always maintains his Shriner-hatted pompousness and overdone formality, even when he takes a prat-fall on the ice or is beaned with a rolling pin by Martha. Life constantly changes but he does not; like a machine, he is unable to adapt.

According to Bergson, "the mechanical encrusted on the living" shows up in three ways: repetition, inversion, and reciprocal interference of series. To begin with, life does not repeat itself; if it is

made to, it is funny. One can even turn a tragedy
into a comedy by sustained repetition of tragic
events; there are comical movies which have murder
after murder, until murder itself becomes a joke (as
in *How to Murder a Rich Uncle*, an old British film in
which the villains are forever mistaking identities
and killing the wrong person). Regarding inversion,
we note that frequently in comic situations there is a
reversal of roles, as when Falstaff plays King Henry
and Prince Hal plays Falstaff. To return to our
mechanical metaphor, machines not only repeat
themselves, they can also be run backwards or up-
side-down. Reciprocal interference of series refers to
two unrelated actions that are made to overlap or
become mixed up in each other. Political cartoons
often use this device, showing for example the presi-
dent on a Hell's-Angels kind of motorcycle labeled
"the economy." Such a picture yokes together the
two "unrelated" worlds of high politics and minor
hoodlumism. All mock-heroic poems are examples of
reciprocal interference of series, throwing together
the incompatible machines of grand epic tradition
and the trivialities of modern life.

These three devices—repetition, inversion, and
interference of series—are the stuff of comedy. But
the satirist frequently resorts to the methods of comedy, and all three devices play a major part in satire.
There is inescapably something machine-like about
the type-characters found in and through the satires
of all periods. A consideration of Bergson might
suitably end with a reminder that he says that the
mechanical as a comic device works only when we
are detached from it. If we have too high an emotional stake in the action or characters, the machine

is no longer funny, as in the tragically inflexible attitudes of the feuding families in *Romeo and Juliet.*

But normally the satirist keeps us at a considerable distance from his characters, so that we have no chance to get to know them well enough to be sympathetic with them. In his chapter on Swift in *The Eighteenth-Century Background,* Basil Willey remarks that to understand everything is to forgive everything, and that he who forgives cannot be a satirist. Thus the writer of satire must forever remain outside his characters. In those intimate moments in *The Rape of the Lock* when we are allowed deep within Belinda's thoughts, satire has temporarily subsided.

When turning to the Augustans to inquire into their views of satire, one immediately notices a much greater continuity than in twentieth-century criticism. In the first place, virtually all of them take the *moral approach* (which, with the exception of Sutherland and a few others, is conspicuously lacking in modern criticism of satire). Dryden, for example, declares that the "most essential" matters in the writing of satire are "the scourging of vice, and exhortation to virtue" *(A Discourse Concerning the Original and Progress of Satire).* John Dennis says that satire is effective in improving manners and attacking crimes (Letter to Matthew Prior, 1721). Addison's famous pronouncement that he intended "to enliven morality with wit, and to temper wit with morality" *(Spectator* 10), certainly echoes the moral view of his forerunners; and later *(Spectator* 249) he was a bit more specific when he stated that the proper use of ridicule was "to laugh men out of vice and folly." Swift, in *Verses on the Death of Dr. Swift,* claims that the public read his works "As with a moral view designed / To cure the vices of mankind." With similar medical imagery (common in talk about satirists' relations to their societies), Pope saw satire as that which "heals with morals what it hurts with wit" *(Epistle to Augustus)*. Later in the period Samuel Johnson's *Dictionary* defined satire as "poems in which wickedness or folly is censured." And sometime after 1780 (the date is uncertain), George Crabbe, who is in many respects the last of the Augustans, was writing that satire is good as long as it fulfills its moral purpose by attacking "the wicked deed" (Crabbe's poem is simply entitled *Satire*). From the foregoing sketch it can be seen that there was a remarkable continuity in Augustan thinking about satire.

Another fairly common sentiment of the period was that proper satire spared the individual and attacked only the *vice and folly* of individuals. But there was an escape clause to the effect that the satirist may directly attack the character of a person when, in Dryden's words, "he is become a public nuisance." Thus libel and lampoon could be seen as serving the noble end of upholding the public morality— for in the context of Augustan society practically any bad man could be seen as a threat to the society at large.

There was also lip service to the effect that one ought to avoid alluding to the opponent's physical properties; yet everyone remembers the "pigmy body" of Shaftesbury in Dryden's *Absalom and Achitophel*, and Lord Hervey who, like a frog, "spits himself abroad" in Pope's *Epistle to Dr. Arbuthnot*. But frequently such literary violence was "justified" on the basis that the target had become a threat to the public.

The amazing thing is that, in this great age of satire, no one of importance troubled himself to work out a really thorough and serious definition of satire. Johnson's definition, mentioned above, is of course lexicographically brief. Dryden was honest enough to admit that satire is elusive of definition, and most of the others seem to have proceeded on the assumption that everyone knew what it was in the first place. Nor is the withering cynicism of Swift much help:

> Satire is a sort of glass, wherein beholders do generally discover everybody's face but their own; which is the chief reason for that kind of reception it meets in the world, and that so very few are offended with it.

But this passage, from the *Preface* to *The Battle of the Books,* is brilliant as satire if not as satiric theory. If one views the shortcomings of modern theories, he can perceive a certain wisdom in this happy negative capability of the eighteenth century. One can learn from the Augustans that the best way to define satire is perhaps not to try to pin it down, but rather hold it open to a large number of possibilities.

The spirit of satire is at least as old as the written word. In the Old Testament one encounters the stern Juvenalian Micah castigating public irreverence, warning the recalcitrants that the Lord "will come down and tread upon the high places of the earth" (1:3). And one meets the frequently Horatian Isaiah, chiding the women who walk with outstretched necks, glancing wantonly with their eyes, mincing along as they go, tinkling with their feet. [3:16]

That the Bible contains significant amounts of satire cannot be denied; but to the neoclassicist, satire really began with the Greek and Roman ancients.

Most neoclassicists assumed that the first genuine satirist was Archilochus, a Greek writer who lived a century or two before the golden age of Athens. According to legend, Archilochus wrote satire so powerful that it caused people to kill themselves. Another important Greek satirist was Aristophanes, who unabashedly practiced the most direct sort of personal attack, frequently alluding to the physical properties of his opponents. His play *The Clouds* satirizes Socrates, and there is a story that when the real Socrates came to see the play he stood up so that the audience could see the difference between the actual man and the buffoon on the stage.

After a less liberal regime came into power in Athens, personal attack became dangerous, and the result was the New Comedy of Menander, Philemon, and Diphilus. The New Comedy dealt with the general rather than the particular. Its satirical purpose, when it had one, was to lash general folly in the form of such type-characters as the parasite, the miser, or the disrespectful servant. Theophrastus practiced essentially the same kind of satire, except in a different form, the prose character, in which type-characters representing vices were held up for public inspection if not ridicule. Thus two important impulses, personal abuse and general attack, were firmly implanted long before the close of the ancient Greek period.

Later, in Rome, the ancient world produced an immense body of satire. The best-known practitioners were Plautus and Terence in the comic drama, Petronius in mixed prose and verse, and Juvenal and Horace in poetry. Only the last two names are of great importance for the student of Augustan poetry. As suggested earlier, they form the two chief spirits or tones of satire in the eighteenth century. Both were extremely popular in the Augustan Age, and critics of the period wrote many words in the effort to describe the temperaments of these two "opposites." Dryden, for instance, wrote that whereas "folly was the proper quarry of Horace, not vice," Juvenal "was wholly employed in lashing vices"; and that Juvenal's "indignation against vice is more vehement" than that of Horace, who merely "laughs to shame all follies." Dennis, following Dryden rather closely, claimed that "Horace argues, insinuates, engages, rallies, smiles; Juvenal exclaims, apostrophizes, exaggerates, lashes, stabs." By the early eighteenth century, then, this dichotomy, artificial as it might have been in some respects, was established. The distinction between the urbane, light Horace and the rather ponderous, almost tragic Juvenal was to remain in the minds of Augustans, almost becoming a cliché, for the rest of the period.

It is important for one who investigates the eighteenth century to keep in mind two kinds of ancient authors. One is the writer as he really was, the other is the Augustan's *image* of him. The real Juvenal, according to twentieth-century scholarship, was far more virulent and nasty than the eight-

eenth century liked to think (for evidence of these
characteristics, the reader is referred to any faithful
translation of Juvenal's Six Satire, "Against
Women," or of the opening of his Ninth Satire). Thus
the Augustans cleaned up Juvenal until he emerged
as a somewhat solemn and dignified English gentleman in the translations by Dryden and the imitations
by Johnson. Indeed, the old pagan was even admitted to the Anglican pulpit, for in the earlier part of
the Augustan period fledgling ministers were urged
to study and use for their sermons the Tenth Satire
("The Vanity of Human Wishes").

There was not so much necessity for cleaning up
Horace; this ancient was fairly polite, even by eighteenth-century standards. But they made him a little
less serious than he had been originally, as if in an
effort to preserve and reinforce the artificial
dichotomy between the Juvenalian and Horatian
traditions. Not all writers, however, went along with
the dichotomy. Pope's *Epilogue to the Satires* sar-
castically scolds Bubb Dodington for assuming that
Horace never grappled with the serious shortcomings of mankind:

> But Horace, sir, was delicate, was nice;
> Bubo observes, he lashed no sort of vice.

But in Pope's time the distinction between Horace
and Juvenal was cheerfully accepted by most
readers.

Turning from antiquity to the Middle Ages, one
finds the spirit of satire still very much alive. There
is real satire in such medieval writings as *Sir Gawain
and the Green Knight* and many parts of Chaucer

(both would be dubbed essentially Horatian by the Augustans), as well as Dante and *Piers the Plowman* (essentially Juvenalian, to the eighteenth century).

In the Renaissance, there is an abundance of satire, but perhaps because the dramas and lyrics of the period overshadow everything, the age is not noted for its satire. Still satire proliferated in the period; one has only to invoke such names as John Skelton, Alexander Barclay, and John Heywood. Later and more relevant to the Augustan Age, came the so-called formal verse satirists of the last decade of the sixteenth century: Donne, John Marston, and Joseph Hall.

In these last three writers, who were essentially Juvenalian in tone, there seems to have been a confusion surrounding the word *satire*. For a time at least, they seemed to think that it came from *satyr*, the rough, shaggy man-goat of mythology, rather than, as was actually the case, from *satura* (a mixed dish or a random collection or hodgepodge—a meaning which was to give license for the casual structures of many satires). Because of the misunderstanding about the derivation of the word, much of the satire of the 1590s exhibits a rough, undisciplined kind of verse, shaggy as a satyr. By the time of Dryden, however, the confusion had long since been cleared up by the French scholar Isaac Casaubon.

It should be mentioned before leaving the Renaissance that this era produced an enormous amount of incidental satire. Parts of *The Faerie Queene*, of *The Arcadia*, and of Shakespeare's plays are examples of strong satire. Specifically, one recalls the assaults on Popery in Spenser (e.g., Errour in Book I) or the many glances at the misuse of the

English language in Shakespeare (e.g., Holofernes, Dogberry, and Osric).

From the time of Dryden to the close of the eighteenth century, satire is in full flower. We will first look at the various forms that satire took, and then we will suggest some reasons for the preponderance of satire in the period.

As mentioned earlier, the Juvenalian and Horatian traditions can be taken to be the two central satiric impulses in the poetry of the eighteenth century. There are dozens of examples but, as is so often the case, only a few have survived as great literature. One thinks of Dryden's translations of Juvenal and of course of Johnson's magnificent renderings, *London* and *The Vanity of Human Wishes.* In the Horatian tradition, the main figure is of course Pope, who late in his career produced *The Satires and Epistles of Horace Imitated.* A lesser figure is Charles Churchill; and a very close parallel in prose to the Horatian poetic tradition is Addison's share of *The Spectator,* light, urbane, conversational, bantering, and directed chiefly against the follies rather than the serious vices of mankind.

Other satiric poetic traditions are the mock-heroic and the burlesque (low style and high subject). Many of the mock-heroic poems of the period have a kind of light Horatian atmosphere about them: *Mac Flecknoe,* Samuel Garth's *The Dispensary, The Rape of the Lock,* and even much of *The Dunciad* in all its versions. Less popular was the burlesque, of which the chief example, Samuel Butler's *Hudibras,* occurs very early in the period.

Other important manifestations of satire occur in prose or drama. Though this work is devoted to po-

etry, a proper treatment of a tradition as important
as satire should touch on all of its forms. One of the
prose satire traditions to produce a classic was fic-
tionalized travel literature, which is one of the
genres that Swift drew on for *Gulliver*. Swift's classic
also drew on another major satirical prose type, the
picaresque tale. This is a satirical narrative usually
having a first person narrator who travels from adventure to adventure. He is as a rule a quick-witted
sort of person who always lands on his feet and functions as a device through which the author can satirize many levels of society. Here and there in the
Augustan period there are a few poems that could be
seen as at least partially picaresque. The most
famous example is *Hudibras*, though here the hero is
less agile than the usual *picaro* or rogue.

Parody too bulked large in the prose and, to a
lesser degree, figured in the poetry (e.g., Gay's
Shepherd's Week). Perhaps the most brilliant writing
of parody in prose was done by Fielding, who twice
took Richardson's *Pamela* to task, once in *Shamela*
and again in the earlier parts of *Joseph Andrews*.
And much later, the all-but-Augustan Jane Austen
was to parody in a general manner the novel of sensibility (in her *Sense and Sensibility*) and the Gothic
school (in her *Northanger Abbey*).

In drama, one can scarcely think of an Augustan
comedy that has survived without thinking of one
containing a great deal of general satire. The great
comedies of manners of the Restoration—*The Country Wife, The Man of Mode, The Way of the World*—
are examples, as well as the second surge, nearly a
hundred years later, that produced *She Stoops to
Conquer* and *The School for Scandal*. In all such

plays, the satire is of that kind that harks back to the New Comedy of Menander and his Roman followers, Plautus and Terence. There are the unmistakable type-characters, all the way from the jealous husband of Menander's *Arbitration* to the gossip-mongers in *The School for Scandal*. The mirror is held up to nature, not to the individual, and general folly is lashed.

In the novel, aside from Fielding and Austen, mentioned above, one can point to large satiric sections in Sterne's *Tristram Shandy*, in Smollett's *Humphrey Clinker*, or in Fanny Burney's *Evelina*. Of all of these, only Sterne, anticipating more recent literature, attacks the customary norm or ideal and defends eccentricity.

The periodical essay also figures in the satiric scene of the eighteenth century. In the foreground, as already suggested, is Mr. Spectator, who was to be successfully echoed later in the century by the more serious *Rambler* of Samuel Johnson. It does not take a shrewd observer to see that satire, much of it brilliant and enduring, is in and through the literature of the Augustan period.

No one will ever know precisely why the eighteenth century identifies itself to succeeding ages as the great time of satire, but one can make some educated guesses. In the first place, there was always the analogy between Augustan Rome and Augustan England; the former had produced great satire, ergo, so did the latter. A less superficial possibility is that many of the eighteenth-century writers, who feared chaos and loved order, saw satire as a means of reinforcing stability and securing the conduct that avoids extremes and practices the Golden Mean.

Anyone who stepped out of the ideal happy medium was suspicious, for England had not so long ago emerged from nearly a century of political and religious strife.

Another possible reason for the great production of satire in the period was that this sort of writing, as Kernan's definition of the private side of the satirist implies, could serve as a kind of safety valve for the release of emotions and strong feelings. Because the lyric had gone underground in the later seventeenth century, there was little opportunity (aside from the ode) for the eighteenth-century poet to wear his heart on his sleeve and escape the doctrine of restraint. Satire could also be seen as an avenue to freedom in diction; for if satire is to attack low targets, it must occasionally employ low language. Again, there is the proposition, almost always true in pre-twentieth-century literature, that satire is didactic; and of course didacticism was extremely popular in the Augustan Age, as may be attested to by the spectacular sales of *The Spectator.*

Still again, a truism seems to be that every society needs a scapegoat; and by the turn of the seventeenth–eighteenth centuries, the traditional image of the Devil, long-vivid in the minds of Christians, had been effectively removed from nature and the universe, chiefly by the empiricism of the New Science. Men had come to believe in a less animistic, more impersonal, and mechanical kind of cosmos. Who then would serve as scapegoat? It is interesting to note that just as the Devil dies, there is a great upsurge in the writing of powerful satire—a kind of writing that by definition cannot exist without targets: patsies, fall guys, and scapegoats of all kinds.

Satire is a hostile sort of art, and perhaps it can be said that the verbal hostility of the Augustans replaced the physical hostility that agonized so much of the seventeenth century. There was also in the eighteenth century the idea, popular but not universal, that since the Fall the world had been undergoing an inexorable decline. Such a decline could not be reversed, much less halted; but a great many seemed to think it could at least be slowed down, and they used satire for this purpose.

Another possible reason for the large body of satire in the period could be that most of the great satirists, as gentlemen of the refined and well-educated upper classes, were conservatives who feared the rising middle class, symbolized by Defoe. Since the Glorious Revolution of 1688–1689 the middle class had been becoming louder in its demand for participation in the cultured world; Grub Street seemed to be encroaching on the polite coffee houses. How else but by satire could refined Augustans stop this insidious, cheapening process? Finally, a reason for all the satire might be that there was a great homogeneity in the period, which meant that conventions were closely defined and that any breaking of convention could be instantly recognized and instantly pounced upon by the paws of satire.

Just as no one can be sure why satire arose at the beginning of the Augustan Age, no one can be certain about the reasons for its waning at the end of the period. But as before, one can make some educated guesses. The "school" of sensibility, though its absurdities could provoke satire, also helped to do away with satire. If man is naturally good, as the sentimentalists believed, then there is little need for satirizing him. Moreover, Augustan satire deals with morals, and in the later eighteenth century, people were beginning to feel that morals were not terribly important as long as one's heart was in the right place. The attitude of benevolence toward one's fellow men, so popular as a doctrine in the late Augustan period, tended to replace the ill-will and hostility on which a great amount of satire is predicated; satire was in effect being "killed with kindness." Also melancholy and gloom, as suitable atmospheres for poetry, were strongly adhered to in the late eighteenth century, and such atmospheres are not as a rule compatible with the wide-awake energies of satire.

Then, too, a number of the satirists had been writers of the aristocratic traditions in literature, and the increasing middle-class audience did not share the aristocratic interest in satire. In the later Augustan Age there is more and more talk about the individual, finally giving way to the extreme egocentricities of the Romantics. But satire almost always uses type-characters, not individuals, and thus it began to make itself irrelevant as the focus shifted to individualism. The middle class was strong in its belief in "progress," a belief that is usually destructive to the motives and aims of the satirist, who must by definition paint a rather unhappy picture of things. Nor did the new audience care as much for didacticism as did the earlier eighteenth-century reader, and didacticism had played a large part in Augustan satire.

Finally, it may be ventured that the deaths of the century's two greatest satirists, Swift and Pope, hastened the decline. After the middle of the 1700s, when both men were dead, there was no one of similar stature to take over.

VI

Some Verse Forms

Although the Augustan Age, like most literary periods, experimented with a great variety of verse forms, it is ordinarily characterized as the era of the heroic couplet. Accordingly, this chapter goes into considerable detail about the couplet. Also treated here are three other verse forms which, though less popular than the couplet, were heavily used in the eighteenth century. These are blank verse, the elegiac or heroic stanza, and the four-stress couplet (including Hudibrastics). The chapter concludes with a few remarks on the Spenserian stanza, a form that is foreign to the Augustan temperament (which craved simplicity) but remarkably persistent in the period.

Heroic Couplet

In English poetry the iambic pentameter rhymed couplet begins with Chaucer, who borrowed the essential ingredients of the form from the fourteenth-century French poet Machaut. But the heroic couplet as the eighteenth century practiced it began in the English Renaissance with such writers as Marlowe, Jonson, Chapman, Drayton, and George Sandys. From the late sixteenth century to the Augustan Age, the heroic couplet gained prestige through the writings of such critics as George Puttenham (*The Art of English Poetry*, 1589); "J. D." (perhaps John Dryden), who wrote a preface for Joshua Poole's *English Parnassus* (1657); and Edward Bysshe (*The Art of English Poetry*, 1702).

The couplet also gained popularity through the poetry of Edmund Waller and Sir John Denham, two later-seventeenth-century writers who are much echoed until the end of the eighteenth century. Indeed, Denham's famed apostrophe to the Thames in his *Cooper's Hill* influenced, for better or worse, every major poet in the Augustan Age. And, as Dryden remarks, the pioneering Waller "first showed us to conclude the sense in distiches." The whole history of the heroic couplet could be generally described as a progressive tightening until Pope, and after that, a progressive loosening until Keats's *Endymion* or, several decades later, Browning's *My Last Duchess* (1842). But to the Augustans, the genuine heroic couplet was the pithy, circumscribed poetry of Pope and of those who either influenced him or were influenced by him.

Not every pair of rhymed iambic pentameter lines is a heroic couplet. (Incidentally, the tag *heroic* derives chiefly from the use of the form in the "heroic plays" of the early Restoration.) The heroic couplet is usually end-stopped; if one merely lets his eyes drift down the right-hand margin of a page of Pope, he will immediately notice the heavy punctuation at the end of each line—units of meaning are fenced off with commas, semicolons, colons, and periods.

If the observer glances down the middle of a page of Pope, he will see more punctuation, whose chief function is to mark off the caesuras within the lines. Well-placed caesuras were one of Pope's criteria for good poetry, though his theory that they should occur after the fourth, fifth, or sixth syllables is frequently at variance with his practice. In any case, the best poets of the period made an effort to place their caesuras with care. Pomfret's *The Choice* (1700), one of the most popular poems of the age, exhibits the orderly architectonics of the caesura: ideal friends should be

> Airy and prudent⊙ merry, but not light;
> Quick in discerning ⊙ and in judging right.
> Secret they should be⊙ faithful to their trust;
> In reasoning cool⊙ strong, temperate and just;
> Obliging, open ⊙ without huffing ⊙ brave,
> Brisk in gay talking⊙ and in sober ⊙ grave.

The circled commas divide each line into groups of syllables that closely correspond with those of the other line of the couplet. Though the Augustan poet characteristically marks the caesura with punctuation, not every caesura is punctuated, and not every mark of punctuation within the line constitutes a caesura.

Another reason why not every pair of rhymed, ten-syllable lines is a heroic couplet is that in the nonheroic couplet the rhyme word is often one of little importance (cf. *Endymion* and *My Last Duchess*).

But Pope and his school felt that the rhyme word ought to have weight and impact, as the passage from Pomfret will demonstrate. Typical of the sentiment of the period is Johnson's remark that, unlike Latin, English is a weak language that needs to be reinforced by "the artifice of rhyme" (Lives of the Poets: Milton). There was also talk about the weight of words within the line. Early critics—Puttenham and Dryden, for example—cautioned against using too many polysyllables; and everyone knows Pope's dictum against the other extreme, "And ten low words oft creep in one dull line," though it has been suggested that what Pope is unknowingly complaining about is too many accents, not too many syllables.

　　　Less easy to interpret is the Augustan concept of strength. Although practically every poet of the period recommended it, virtually no one explained it. It seems to mean a virtue of two ingredients: great compression and tight syntactical connection. Denham was felt to be the best example; and when writers commented on his strength, they no doubt had in mind his passage on the Thames:

> O could I flow like thee, and make thy stream
> My great example, as it is my theme!
> Though deep, yet clear, though gentle,
> 　　yet not dull,
> Strong without rage, without o'er-flowing full.

The ideal writer was one who combined strength and sweetness, another slightly difficult term, which seems to mean mellifluousness, a smooth flow. The great example of sweetness was Waller, Denham's fellow pioneer in the heroic couplet.

As already suggested, syntax plays an important part in the heroic couplet. One of the most common syntactical patterns used by the Augustans is parallelism; that is, repetition of grammatical patterns rather than of words.

Ye shady beeches, and ye cooling streams,
Defence from Phoebus', not from Cupid's beams,
To you I mourn, nor to the deaf I sing,
The woods shall answer, and their echo ring.

That this passage from Pope's *Pastorals* ("Summer") is as regular and orderly as a pavilion can be seen in the following parsing:

noun phrase (and) noun phrase
noun: prepositional phrase (not) prepositional
    phrase
indirect object: subject verb (nor) subject verb
subject verb (and) subject verb.

Such regularized syntax is part of the image of order and decorum so much worshipped by the Augustans. The other side of the image, however, is chaos and rage; the same kind of parallelism could be used to throw these into high relief, as in Crabbe's description of idle card players—"Grave without sense, and pointed without wit" (*The Borough*, X)—or Johnson's version of Restoration comedy—"Intrigue was plot, obscenity was wit" (*Prologue ... in Drury Lane*). Within the confines of his syntactical regularity, then, the Augustan poet could achieve a great excitement and tension. He could point the moral finger at folly or vice and at the same time imply the ideal norm of order. He could do the same thing through the use of chiasmus, a kind of inverted syntax in which the second statement reverses the grammar of the first: "Live unregarded, unlamented die" (Johnson's *London*).

Another frequently used device is antithesis, which involves the juxtaposing or balancing of opposites. Crabbe, for example, wanted to describe pastoral life "As *truth* will paint it, and as *bards* will not" *(The Village)* and Goldsmith's more idealized *Deserted Village* has images of rustic games, "The *young* contending as the *old* surveyed." Antithetical statements are effective when forced into close parallelism, as when Dryden declares "That vice triumphs, and virtue suffers here" *(Religio Laici)*. Antitheses often imply the Golden Mean; Pomfret, whose poem *The Choice* is constructed around the idea, calls for friends who are "airy and prudent" — the proper behavior is the middle course between these two opposites. It is important to notice that this antithetical wit of the Augustans is not the unresolved paradox of the Metaphysical poets. When Pope calls for a critic who is "Modestly bold and humanly severe," he is positing a middle road, not an insoluble dilemma (*Essay on Criticism*, III). And even the many paradoxes about man's middle position in the universe in the *Essay on Man* are not finally paradoxes because, by the end of the poem, Pope has furnished a solution which is a balanced conduct of good sense and modesty.

The above paragraphs suggest that a major poetic problem for the Augustan was achieving variety and vigor within a tight and limited framework. One solution was to end the line with a climax.

According to Dryden's *Absalom and Achitophel,*
Zimri (the Duke of Buckingham) "Was chymist, fid-
dler, statesman and buffoon." The satirist's victim
rises through a hierarchy of occupations, each more
respectable than the one before it, until he is climac-
tically—or anticlimactically—dropped to the lowest
rank of "buffoon." Or the climax may occur before
the end of the line, as in the incongruous Bibles on
Belinda's dressing table, which is piled high with
"Puffs, powders, patches, Bibles, billet-doux" *(The
Rape of the Lock).* Sometimes the climactic structure
spreads itself through both halves of the couplet, as
in the *Essay on Criticism* (I):

> Some have at first for wits, then poets passed,
> Turned critics next, and proved plain fools
>   at last.

The sententiousness of the heroic couplet is
caused by a number of factors, some already discussed. Two more devices aiding compression are
syncope and ellipsis. Syncope is a contraction, an
omitting of a vowel or consonant sound to reduce the
number of syllables (e.g., "o'er", "heav'n"). Ellipsis is
an omission of grammar. There are a number of
ellipses in the satires of Charles Churchill: "To make
the oath was rash; to keep it, sin" *(The Prophecy of
Famine: a Scotch Pastoral);* but they can be found
anywhere in the Augustan poets—"To err is human;
to forgive, divine" (*Essay on Criticism,* II).

As indicated above, the heroic couplet has its
own structure; it is finished, polished, and self-suffi-
cient. A couplet can often stand by itself as a complete poem or epigram, and it was sometimes meant

to. An example is Pope's epitaph on Newton, quoted here in full:

> Nature and nature's laws lay hid in night;
> God said, *Let Newton be!* and all was light.

No one will ever know exactly why the heroic couplet came to the fore in the Augustan Age. One should first admit the possibility that there are *no* reasons for the phenomenon, or that it was a matter of mere fashion. After that, it is safe to make some educated guesses. One possibility is that the couplet, with its equal division into two lines (and often into halves of lines), was a good vehicle for expressing the compromise of the Golden Mean. It could also be suggested that it matched the eighteenth-century sense of orderly certainty, the tendency of the period to sum up, aphorize, circumscribe, restrain, epigrammatize.

There was also the feeling, expressed by Johnson and others, that the loose syntactical and casual phonetic nature of English called for a tight framework of meter and rhyme. This attitude derived from the Augustan's habit of comparing himself with his ancient counterparts of Rome and (less frequently) Greece; thus it can be said that the ancients had a hand in shaping the couplet. Indeed, the "elegiacs" of Ovid and the diction of Virgil frequently anticipate the eighteenth century. And in sixteenth-century England, Sidney, Spenser, and others were busy trying to impose classical meters upon the restiveness and unpredictable variety of English. Another reason for the popularity of the heroic couplet in the eighteenth century was that it early came to be associated with the "heroic," with dignity and politeness, the cultured and the civilized; it matched very well the Augustan's image of himself as first of all a highly civilized and social creature.

Further, the heroic couplet had the impetus of having been exploited, early in the period, by two brilliant artists, Dryden and Pope; this was enough to thrust Milton's prestigious blank verse aside for a number of decades. And what blank verse there was frequently shows the unmistakable influence of the terse and sharp-edged couplet; the most extreme example is Johnson's *Irene*, but the influence can also be seen in the un-Miltonic haltings of Young's *Night Thoughts* and, to a lesser degree, in Thomson's *Seasons*. Not until late in the period with Cowper's *The Task* does blank verse begin to escape the couplet. But there was never again a mellifluous Milton.

The heroic couplet was a major poetic form for a century and a half. It would be less than honest, however, to suggest that it was the *only* major form. It is too easy to forget that much of the best work of the period was done in other measures: Butler's *Hudibras*, Gay's *Fables*, Thomson's *The Seasons*, Gray's *Elegy*, Collins's *Ode to Evening*, and of course the lyrics of Smart, Burns, and Blake. All of these are reminders of the great variety of Augustan poetry, of which the heroic couplet was only an important part.

Blank Verse

Blank verse (unrhymed iambic pentameter) is widespread in the Augustan Age. This proclamation may startle newcomers to the period, especially if they have been brought up under the inaccurate cliché that the age was purely one of "reason" and heroic couplets. But blank verse is one of the most traveled roads in the realm of eighteenth-century literature. For one thing, practically every serious drama from the late Restoration to 1800 employed the form. Dryden had set the standard by a declaration of independence from the use of rhyme in drama in the preface to his tragedy *All for Love* (1678):

> In my style, I have professed to imitate the divine Shakespeare; which that I might perform more freely, I have disencumbered myself from rhyme.

Dryden was reacting against the "heroic play," popular in the early Restoration. This was a species of drama in which the audience was subjected to hours of ranting couplets about love and honor; in which "Declamation roared while passion slept," as Samuel Johnson put it *(Prologue ... in Drury Lane)*.

Even if one excludes the drama from his survey of eighteenth-century blank verse, he is still confronted with a mass of poetry using the form. It is noteworthy, too, that many of the most widely read and popular blank-verse pieces of the era were composed by writers of major stature. One has only to think of such efforts as Young's *Night Thoughts*, Thomson's *The Seasons*, or Cowper's *The Task*. And there were numerous blank verse writings by minor figures; one scholar has counted approximately a thousand such poems appearing from 1700 to 1800, and no one knows how many others were lost or

never published. It should also be mentioned that the
great couplet writers who frowned on non-dramatic
blank verse still felt it to be appropriate for play writing. Even Johnson, who once scornfully asked,
"When was blank verse without pedantry?" (Lives of
the Poets: Aikenside), used blank verse in his tragedy
Irene.

Irene was not successful. The reason, or at least
part of the reason, is not far to seek, for the blank
verse of Irene is little more than unrhymed heroic
couplets that miss the point and spirit of true blank
verse, which is the kind of flowing freedom achieved
in the later plays of Shakespeare and in Milton's
longer poems. Here, on the other hand is the choppi-
ness of Johnson:

> What plagues, what tortures, are in store
>   for thee,
> Thou sluggish idler, dilatory slave?
> Behold the model of consummate beauty,
> Torn from the mourning earth by thy neglect.
>   [V.xiii]

Clearly there is a dilemma here; the failure of the
heroic or couplet play, plus the blank-verse failure
evinced by Johnson's halting lines, makes it apparent that the Augustans lacked a suitable vehicle
for serious poetic drama. With the exceptions of
Dryden's All for Love and Otway's Venice Preserved,
there is scarcely a first-rate blank verse drama from
1660 to 1800.

That the couplet, a successful form in its own
right, adversely affected the blank verse of the
Augustan Age can be seen in any number of works;

too often one finds the orderly architectonics of antithesis, parallelism, and end-stop inhibiting the
freedom of the lines. In Young's *Night Thoughts*, for
example, the reader frequently comes across couplet
thinking in blank-verse language; here the poet
ruminates upon the predicament of man:

> Milk and a swathe at first his whole demand,
> His whole domain at last a turf or stone,
> To whom, between, a world may seem too
>   small.
>
> ["Night the First"]

And sometimes in Young a single line is a poem in itself: "Procrastination is the thief of time." Surely
such aphoristic rounding out of the thought does not
contribute to the kind of verse in which the sense is
"variously drawn out."

Similar problems can be seen in such popular
works as Thomson's *Seasons*, Aikenside's *Pleasures
of the Imagination*, and Joseph Warton's *The En-
thusiast*, though admittedly these poems are a little
more flowing than *Night Thoughts*. It is not really until Cowper's *The Task* that something of the genuine
Miltonic flow is revived, and even here no serious
student would equate Cowper with Milton. The lover
of eighteenth-century poetry must admit that truly
first-rate non-dramatic blank verse simply does not
occur between Milton and the great Romantics.

Much of the trouble would seem to lie in the use
of syntax. Milton had the trick of often refusing to let
the natural breaks between phrases and clauses occur at the end of the line—the reader must, as it were,
hold the note until well into the next line. But in the

Augustan's blank verse, the line characteristically terminates with the end of a syntactical unit, as can be seen in the above quotations from Johnson and Young. Even when the poet tried to imitate Milton closely, the results were still choppy, as in John Philips's *Splendid Shilling*, a poem humorous in its subject but deadly serious in its efforts to imitate Milton's style.

A history of blank verse must of course go back beyond the music of Milton and Shakespeare. The form first made its way into English in a translation of part of Virgil's *Aeneid* by Henry Howard, Earl of Surrey, in the earlier sixteenth century. (Blank verse was first developed by the Italians and was called *versi sciolti*, i.e., "verses set free".) In England it was first used in drama in the tragedy *Gorboduc* (1561) by Thomas Norton and Thomas Sackville. With Marlowe and then Shakespeare, blank verse became the standard form for serious drama.

It was not until Milton that blank verse was successfully exploited for non-dramatic poetry. This great poet justified his use of a non-rhyming measure in the preface to *Paradise Lost:*

> The measure of [*Paradise Lost*] is English heroic verse without rime, as that of Homer in Greek, and of Virgil in Latin; rhyme being no necessary adjunct or true ornament of poem or good verse, in longer works especially, but the invention of a barbarous age, to set off wretched matter and lame meter.

There is an irony here, in that the earlier eighteenth century, which abhorred most things Gothic or medieval, should be so fond of rhyme. The irony is even more puzzling when one reflects that Milton and the Augustans are actually starting from the same assumption: that the ancient Greeks and Romans represented the high point in human development and that the "barbarous age" or Middle Ages were the low point. But the problem is solved when one reflects that the Augustans felt that they could "strengthen" the looseness of English through the use of rhyme and thus imitate the ancients; indeed, it is the implication of Johnson's pronouncements on *Paradise Lost* that Milton, by abandoning rhyme, was *not enough* like the ancients. English, naturally weak and capricious in its syntax, had to be beefed up by rhyme so that it could somehow resemble the tight strength and syntax of Latin and Greek.

With exceptions in drama, blank verse tended to go underground in the later seventeenth century, though it remained very much a matter of critical argument. In the early eighteenth century, the form began to come into fairly wide use again, but it is significant that no major non-dramatic poet from Milton to Thomson did anything with it. Blank verse was being written, but the great masters from Milton to Thomson were busy with the couplet.

In the middle of the eighteenth century, the production of blank verse begins to rise, due in part to the immense success of *The Seasons* and due also in part to a general reaction against the couplet, which had by then a very long tenure. There was a push for "freedom," and writers thought that to be free from the doctrine of restraint was to quit rhyming. But as illustrated earlier, the freedom was illusory; for most of the blank verse of the eighteenth century is imprisoned in the syntax of the couplet. It may be appropriate to end with a line from John Byrom's *Thoughts on Rhyme and Blank Verse:* "A blockhead's a blockhead, with rhyme, or without."

Elegiac or Heroic Stanza

The elegiac or heroic stanza consists of four lines of iambic pentameter ryhming *abab*. This volume includes a note on the form chiefly because there seems to be some confusion in the modern reader's mind—and in the eighteenth-century mind—about the names *elegiac* and *heroic* as applied to this stanza. One thing is clear: Sometime between Dryden's *Heroick Stanzas* on Cromwell and William Lisle Bowles's *Elegiac Stanzas Written During Sickness at Bath,* the poet's attitude toward the form had changed; for both Dryden and Bowles are using the same stanza form. Actually, the above is a bit of an exaggeration because it did not take the length of time between Dryden and Bowles (more than a century) to bring about a change. At least as early as Gray's *Elegy Written in a Country Churchyard* (perhaps begun as early as 1742), and possibly as early as Gay's *Elegiac Epistle to a Friend* (ca. 1732), the iambic pentameter quatrain rhyming *abab* was most often associated with elegy. After this there are any number of elegies written in the "elegiac stanza" form; some of the better ones were done by Beattie, Chatterton, Shenstone, and Bowles.

But a hundred years earlier, it was natural for Dryden to call the form *heroic,* and just as natural for Davenant to choose the form for his heroic poem *Gondibert.* These earlier writers saw the heroic stanza as fit for high matters of love and honor, whereas the later poets saw it as fit for mourning. Perhaps the shift to the latter attitude can be symbolized by *Stanzas,* a piece done early in the eighteenth century by John Sheffield, Earl of Mulgrave. Mulgrave's poem seems to walk the line between a quiet, melancholy tendency and the high matter of state, insofar as that is possible. His topic is the difficulty of public service in his era, but he seems to move close to the melancholy of Gray. Having discoursed upon the dangers of public service, the poet concludes in this manner:

> Who knows but my example then may please
> Such noble, hopeful spirits as appear
> Willing to slight their pleasures, and their ease,
> For fame and honor? Till at last they hear,

> After much trouble borne, and danger run,
> The crown assisted, and my country served;
> Without good fortune I had been undone,
> Without a good estate I might have starved.

(Incidentally, it is unusual to see one stanza run-on into another, at least in the Augustan handling of the form). Certainly there is melancholy and incipient elegy in Mulgrave's tone, but just as certain is the presence of heroic sentiment and atmosphere. In Mulgrave one can view evolution in action.

The above is not to suggest that the evolution was clearcut. Gray's posthumous and unfinished *Stanzas to Mr. Bentley* is very public and proclamatory in tone, and takes literary criticism for its subject. Then again, Goldsmith's *Stanzas on the Taking of*

Quebec, and Death of General Wolfe is at once very elegiac and very heroic:

> Amidst the clamor of exulting joys,
> Which triumph forces from the patriot heart,
> Grief dares to mingle her soul-piercing voice,
> And quells the raptures which from pleasure
>   start.

And about the same time, Shenstone referred to the form as "heroic meter" *(A Prefatory Essay on Elegy)*. The only fair conclusion to make would seem to be that even though the stanza form tends to shift from heroic to elegiac, there lingers until late in the period a definite confusion between the two. Perhaps it was there at the outset, for, as early as Sir John Davies's *Nosce Teipsum* (1599), lyricism, philosophy, melancholy, and heroism get along well together in the same four-line, iambic pentameter, *abab* scheme.

Four-Stress Couplet and Hudibrastics

The iambic tetrameter couplet was almost as commonly used in the eighteenth century as the heroic couplet. It is difficult to make distinctions within this simple form, but perhaps one can construct a spectrum ranging from the heavy use of caesura to the virtual lack of caesura. After that, one can add still another dimension, the Hudibrastic.

Most of the iambic four-stress couplets of the eighteenth century lean toward one end of the spectrum, that of the galloping verse that is, for the most part, unimpeded by pauses. The most notable practitioners of this meter were Swift and Gay, but it appears in the fables of many writers throughout the period. It seems especially suited for narrative. Here is an example of the running four-stress line of Swift:

> A bitch that was full pregnant grown,
> By all the dogs and curs in town;
> Finding her ripened time was come,
> Her litter teeming from her womb,
> Went here and there, and everywhere,
> To find an easy place to lay-her.

The passage is from the *Fable of the Bitches*, in which occur very few real pauses of the sort in the fifth line just quoted.

The other extreme of the spectrum is the kind of tetrameter couplet that is so slowed down by pauses as almost to fall into shorter sections of half-lines. The best example occurs not in the Augustan Age but earlier, in the magnificent *Exequy* of Henry King:

> Dear loss! since thy untimely fate
> My task hath been to meditate
> On thee, on thee; thou art the book,
> The library whereon I look,
> Though almost blind. For thee, loved clay,
> I languish out, not live, the day.

The extremely halting quality is quite appropriate for King's sobbing grief over the early death of his wife.

The middle of the spectrum is best exemplified by the quiet control of Andrew Marvell, whose *To His Coy Mistress* uses carefully selected pauses to add dignity to the message:

Had we but world enough, and time,
This coyness, lady, were no crime.
We would sit down, and think which way
To walk, and pass our long love's day.

The effect is not the haltingness of King, nor the galloping of Swift, but a kind of happy compromise between the two.

On the other hand, it should not be assumed that the Augustan lacked the talent shown by King and Marvell. Swift, in moving away from the narrative towards the lyrical, can exhibit some of the great Marvellian control:

Oh, would it please the gods, to split
Thy beauty, size, and years, and wit;
No age could furnish out a pair
Of nymphs so graceful, wise and fair.

This passage, from *On Stella's Birthday*, also follows the expertise of Marvell and King in occasionally allowing the sense to be "variously drawn out" into the next line.

Of course, one has to measure the poet by what he is trying to do in the poem; and most of the time the Augustans are not especially interested in the peculiar modulated lyricism that was so popular in the earlier or mid-seventeenth century. But one could wish for more of the Marvellian music in the Augustans, and wish for less of the nonfunctional galloping of, say, *Verses on the Death of Dr. Swift*.

At the beginning of the discussion it was suggested that, in addition to the above-described spectrum, another dimension could be added—that of the Hudibrastic. This species of iambic tetrameter couplet, made famous by Samuel Butler's early Restoration burlesque piece *Hudibras*, is distinguished not so much by any peculiarities of meter as by eccentricities in rhyme. For Butler's rhythm is generally of the unimpeded type that anticipates Swift and the fable writers. The poet states that the "Argument" of *Hudibras* will involve

> Sir Hudibras his passing worth,
> The manner how he sallied forth,
> His arms and equipage, are shown;
> His horse's virtues and his own.
> The adventure of the bear and fiddle
> Is sung, but breaks off in the middle.

And as the poem gets underway, the reader is frequently bombarded with comic rhymes:

> Then did Sir Knight abandon dwelling,
> And out he rode a-colonelling.

There are dozens of poems throughout the Augustan Age written in "Hudibrastics"—so title pages claim—but most of them are, like the original, Swiftian tetrameters with the addition of comic rhymes.

Spenserian Stanza

The Spenserian stanza, rhyming *ababbcbcc*, consists of eight lines of iambic pentameter and a final hexameter or Alexandrine line, the two halves of the Alexandrine usually being divided by a caesura. The form was invented by Spenser, whose *Faerie Queene* was published by 1596. Possibly due to the intricacies and limits of its rhyme scheme, the Spenserian stanza has never been widely practiced; but a few major figures—including Byron, Shelley, Keats, and Tennyson—have used it well. The most important eighteenth-century poets to write seriously in this form were Shenstone *(The Schoolmistress)*, Thomson *(The Castle of Indolence)*, and Burns *(The Cotter's Saturday Night)*. Early in his career Pope wrote a few comic Spenserian stanzas *(The Alley)*. This form, then, is not one of the major tendencies of eighteenth-century verse, and as late as 1795 William Roscoe was attacking Spenser for fettering himself with a complex stanza-scheme (*Life of Lorenzo de' Medici*, I). On the other hand, poems written in Spenserian or near-Spenserian stanzas appear on an approximate average of every dozen years from 1600 to 1800. Although he was not widely imitated in the period, Spenser was highly thought of by many, including his satirizer, Pope. At the height of his career Pope once said, "I read the *Faerie Queene* when I was about twelve, with a vast deal of delight; and I think it gave me as much when I read it over about a year or two ago [Spence, *Anecdotes*]" Pope's view is not highly unusual—it was just that many eighteenth-century poets admired Spenser without wishing to imitate him.

The eighteenth century, then, is an age of heroic couplets; but as suggested by the foregoing discussion of verse forms, the Augustan Age is also much more than that.

VII

Backgrounds, Intellectual and Literary

The purpose of this chapter is to furnish a series of sketches of major concepts and events in the literary and intellectual life of the Augustan period. The following matters are discussed: the Great Chain of Being; the Golden Mean; Reason; Augustan "rules" for writing in the genres; imitation; some directions in the criticism of poetry in the eighteenth century; the ancient-modern quarrel; some differences between the Augustans and the Romantics; the transition from the earlier seventeenth century (or "Metaphysical" period) to the Augustan Age.

The Great Chain of Being

The great Chain of Being originated in Plato's *Timaeus*, achieved some popularity in the Middle Ages, became more popular in the Renaissance, and reached its apex in the Augustan Age, especially in the early 1700s. It is a world view in which creation is seen as a continuous scale or chain of existence, ex-

tending from the lowliest creature, up through the
more complicated animals, through man (who is in
the middle of the chain), through the ranks of the
angels, reaching finally to God Himself.

The "logic" of those who embraced the doctrine
of the Chain of Being may be explained in terms of
three sub-doctrines: plenitude, continuity, and gradation. *Plenitude* is the belief that the universe is *full;*
because God is benevolent and because He joys in
creating, He created to the maximum extent possible, peopling the cosmos with all the life that it could
contain. It follows, then, that the universe is one of
continuity—there are no gaps; precisely where one
level of existence ends, another begins. The third
sub-doctrine, *gradation,* is based on the belief that
God is orderly, somewhat like a kindly supernatural
architect or watchmaker. Such a God would of course
construct his universe in neat ranks, rather than let
chaos rule. Indeed, it was felt that if even one link in
the Great Chain were broken or dislocated, the entire cosmos would be threatened.

In the First Epistle of his *Essay on Man,* Pope
gave eloquent expression to the ideas discussed
above:

> See through this air, this ocean, and this
>   earth,
> All matter quick, and bursting into birth.
> Above, how high, progressive life may go!
> Around, how wide! how deep extend below!
> Vast chain of being! which from God began,
> Natures ethereal, human, angel, man,
> Beast, bird, fish, insect, what no eye can see,
> No glass can reach; from infinite to thee,
> From thee to nothing.—On superior powers

Were we to press, inferior might on ours:
Or in the full creation leave a void,
Where, one step broken, the great scale's
     destroyed:
From nature's chain whatever link you strike,
Tenth or ten thousandth, breaks the chain
     alike.
     And, if each system in gradation roll,
Alike essential to the amazing whole,
The least confusion but in one, not all
That system only, but the whole must fall.

As can be inferred, the doctrine of the Great Chain of Being had serious philosophical and religious implications for the eighteenth-century. Though it might be assumed that the middle of the Chain would be an ideal place, most Augustans saw man's mid-scale position as far from comfortable. In *Spectator* 519, Addison concluded

that he, who in one respect is associated with angels and arch-angels, may look upon a Being of infinite perfection as his Father and the highest order of spirits as his brethren, and may in another respect say to *Corruption, thou art my father, and to the worm, thou art my mother and my sister.*

Moreover, man's pride caused him to be forever dissatisfied with his middle state. Half-animal, half-angel, he had since the Fall arrogantly tried to struggle upward, only to be thrust back down to subhuman gracelessness. Wise men knew that the center of the universe was no place to be.

It can also be inferred that the doctrine of the

Great Chain had far-reaching political implications.
If God had constructed the universe in the form of a
static hierarchy, it was only logical to assume that
man should imitate the hierarchy in his politics.
Thus, in the earlier 1700s, man as a socio-political
creature is frequently exhorted to know and
acknowledge his place, and to refrain from aspiring
upward. Pope's *Essay on Man* is relevant once again:

> Honor and shame from no condition rise;
> Act well your part, there all the honor lies.
> Fortune in men has some small difference made,
> One flaunts in rags, one flutters in brocade.
>   [The Fourth Epistle]

It should be added, however, that some Augustans—
notably Dr. Johnson—could believe in social and political subordination without believing specifically
in the Great Chain of Being. Johnson's reason for not
believing in the Chain was that there simply was not
enough evidence to support the idea. One had only
to step outside and look about the creation; immediately he would notice the many gaps between
species or ranks.

The Great Chain also had some literary implications. Among critics of the turn of the seventeenth
and eighteenth centuries, there was a persistent
habit of ranking the various poetic genres or kinds.
Epic and tragedy normally appeared at the top,
while the less dignified types, like pastoral, took
their place near the bottom. Lowest of all were such
"mean" traditions as epigram and satire.

The Chain of Being, popular in the age of Pope,
was by and large incompatible with the revolution-

ary tendencies of the second half of the century. The Romantics steadily undermined the concept, making it more fluid and dynamic and less static. But it was left to the Victorian Age to furnish the Great Chain's ultimate antithesis—this was of course the concept of Evolution.

The Golden Mean

An age so much in love with order was quick to embrace the ancient doctrine of the Golden Mean. Its first major formulation appears in Aristotle's *Nichomachean Ethics;* but as far as the Augustans were concerned, the chief classical exponent of the *via media* or "middle way" was Horace. A persistent underlying theme in Horace's *Satires* and *Epistles* is that for every virtue there are two vices, both of which are extremes. Thus courage is a virtue achieved by steering the middle course: too little courage is cowardice; too much is foolhardiness. The doctrine of the Golden Mean is essentially one of temperance, moderation, and conservatism; and it is interesting to speculate about the way history might have gone if all men had settled for the golden compromise. It is probably safe to say that without such celebrated "extremists" as Christ, Columbus, Galileo, and Marx, the world would have changed very little—for better or for worse.

The Golden Mean was especially popular in England in the late seventeenth and early eighteenth centuries. The politico-religious strife of the 1640s and the social turbulence of the early Restoration years (1660s and 1670s) were fresh in the memories of Englishmen, and the call for moderation and stability was often heard. This meant compromise, and compromise meant the Golden Mean. Dryden posited the Aristotelian-Horatian ideal in his satire *The Medal:*

> Our temperate isle will no extremes sustain
> Of popular sway or arbitrary reign
> But slides between them both into the best;
> Secure in freedom, in a monarch blest.

And in *Spectator* 10 Addison called for a balance between a different pair of opposites—he wished to "enliven morality with wit, and temper wit with morality." The most sustained poetic expression of the Golden Mean is John Pomfret's *The Choice;* but it remained for Pope to give the most pithy and compressed expressions to the idea. In his *Essay on Criticism,* for example, he wrote that a good critic should be "modestly bold and humanly severe," achieving an extreme of compression through the use of oxymora or contradictions in terms. The ideal critic should travel the middle road between modesty and boldness, gentleness and severity. However, by the mid-1700s the Golden Mean began to be undermined by a new fashion of the radical and the drastic—so that by the 1740s it was possible for Collins in his *Ode to Simplicity* to refer to "divine excess." The ultimate and final destruction of the Golden Mean occurred in the revolutionary atmosphere of the end of the century.

Though the Golden Mean may be expressed in any verse form, it is most commonly found in the heroic couplet. It may have been the couplet's closed, two-line structure, its antithetical tendency, and its habitual use of mid-line caesuras that made it especially appropriate for singing the *via media*.

Reason

An age in love with order is not necessarily a rationalistic age. Only the uninitiated could refer to the Augustan period as an "age of reason." The truth is that virtually all eighteenth-century men of letters had strong reservations and doubts about man's rational faculties. In his *Satire Against Mankind*, the Earl of Rochester referred to reason as an elusive "*ignis fatuus* of the mind." Dryden attacked reason in his *Religio Laici*, chiefly on the grounds that it was the product of mortal or "finite" existence and therefore inadequate in the really important parts of man's existence (i.e., religion, faith, and the world to come). In his *Essay on Man* Pope vindicated God and the cosmos by declaring that in "spite of pride, in erring reason's spite, / One truth is clear: WHATEVER IS, IS RIGHT." One of the most extreme statements against reason was made by the philosopher Hume in his *Treatise of Human Nature*, Book II: "Reason is, and ought to be, the slave of the passions, and can never pretend to any other office than to serve and obey them." Hume is clearly in the wave of the future, for the elevation of feeling over reason is a main tendency of later eighteenth-century writers and, after them, the Romantics.

The earlier Augustans, however, were opposed to only one type of reason; there was another kind that they upheld. The "*ignis fatuus*," which Rochester finds so odious, is speculative reason, the kind that the projectors in Book III of *Gulliver's Trav-*

els are using in their efforts to extract sunbeams out of cucumbers. It was this kind of reason, used in wasteful, vain intellectual or philosophical pursuits, that the Augustans so heartily eschewed. But they just as heartily defended what Rochester calls "right reason." Some synonyms for this more mundane and more defensible sort of reason would be: "practical reason," "plain reason," "good sense," or "common sense."

The chief use of this faculty lay in coming to terms with society, in harmoniously functioning in the world. "Right reason," then, in order to cater to society, had to exercise a good deal of control over the passions. In the ideal Augustan world order, there was little room for any kind of intemperate outburst. The major function of passion, according to Pope's *Essay on Man* (Epistle II), was to provide energy for the purposes of right reason: passion is the "gale" that fills the sails and drives the ship of man, but reason is the "card"—i.e., the navigating device—which provides direction for the energies of the feelings.

In spite of their skepticism about reason, the Augustans talked about it a great deal. So much so, that a useful antidote for the modern reader is George Santayana's contention that reason is nothing more than one of the "inherited passions," which voraciously seeks consistency and order to the exclusion of everything else.

Rules

The eighteenth century seems to exude a sense of carefully controlled order, and in reading

Augustan poetry one often receives the impression that for each genre there is a certain set of rules, usually derived from classical authors. Thus, for the epic, one would follow the examples of Homer and Virgil; for the ode, Pindar and Horace; for the pastoral, Theocritus and Virgil; for the epigram, Martial—and so forth. Moreover, eighteenth-century critics produced a number of essays spelling out the rules in detail. Dryden's Preface to *Albion and Albanius*, for example, lays down the rules for writing opera; and his *Essay Concerning the Original and Progress of Satire* offers some dos and don'ts for that type of writing. Pope's *Discourse on Pastoral Poetry* does the same for pastoral. *Spectator* 618 gives rules for writing Ovidian (i.e., heroic) epistles and Horatian epistles. Congreve outlines the procedures for writing Pindaric odes in the preface to his *Ode to Queen Anne*. In *Guardian* 16, Steele comments on the proper way to write a song; and later in the century, Dr. Johnson writes *An Essay on Epitaphs*, which dictates the right manner and content for tombstone verse.

On the other hand, it is important to stress that virtually no serious Augustan was completely in favor of rules. For as often as one can find rules-criticism (as those named above), one can find criticism *attacking* the rules—sometimes by the very author of a piece of rules-criticism. Thus, although Johnson had legislated the epitaph, in his *Preface to Shakespeare* he attacked the time-honored rule of unity of place by suggesting that if one can imagine the stage to be anything other than what it is, one can imagine it to be any place or places. Many other Augustans also voiced skepticism about the rules. Sir

William Temple, though very much a conservative, declared that "there is something in the genius of poetry too libertine to be confined to so many rules." Dryden attacked French playwrights for their "servile observations of the unities of time and place." Charles Gildon wrote that "an English audience will never be pleased with a dry, jejune and formal method that excludes variety, as the religious observation of the rules of Aristotle does." John Dennis asked, rhetorically, "what man who had common sense ever affirmed that the perfection of all good poetical writings was owing to rules alone?" Addison stated that "there is sometimes a greater judgement shown in deviating from the rules of art than in adhering to them." But as with Johnson, Addison could also make concessions to the rules, as he did in the series of *Spectators* on *Paradise Lost,* in which he frequently invokes the rules of epic. More than one Augustan wished to have it both ways.

It is a favorite contention of earlier literary historians that the incipient Romanticism of the later eighteenth century was instrumental in causing the great rule-bound edifice of neoclassicism to come crashing to earth. But as we have seen, the Augustans were skeptical about the rules in the first place. Secondly, what happens toward the end of the century is not so much a removing of rules as a replacing of old rules with new ones. A prime example is the doctrine of the sublime, which in some ways seems more hidebound and restrictive than many earlier Augustan doctrines. Nor would it be extravagant to suggest that there are rules (e.g., about diction) in Wordsworth's *Preface to the Lyrical Ballads,* which is so often viewed as a literary Declaration of Independence.

The truth seems to be that no literary age ever fails to impose rules on itself; and the basic question is not "are there rules?" but rather "what form do the rules take?" At the present time, the rules seem to take an unwritten form, as in a recent anthology that contains not one single poem that rhymes. There may be less honesty in such an approach to the rules than in the sometimes too-blatant asseverations of the Augustan critics.

Imitation

Dr. Johnson, accustomed to uttering epigrams about the profession of letters, once wrote that "no man was ever great by imitation" (*Rasselas,* Chapter X). This axiom should be taken with a grain of salt, for Johnson is using the word here in only one of its two major Augustan meanings. He is referring to imitation in the sense of slavishly copying or dully reproducing the original; it is this sense that has survived and come down to the twentieth century. In Johnson's time, however, "imitation" could also mean a highly creative act, as he himself knew when he called his famous poem, *London,* an imitation of Juvenal's Third Satire. Even the casual reader of these ancient and modern pieces can see that Johnson uses Juvenal merely as a point of departure for his own imagination. Whereas Juvenal's attack was launched against ancient Rome, Johnson's is against eighteenth-century London; and Johnson fills his poem with attitudes and images that could never have occurred to Juvenal. Imitation in eighteenth-century England, then, was by no means a slavish or unoriginal business.

One can further his understanding of eighteenth-century imitation by placing it in the context of "translation." Here it is illuminating to turn to Dryden's *Preface Concerning Ovid's Epistles:*

> All translation, I suppose, may be reduced to these three heads: First, that of metaphrase, or turning an author word by word, and line by line, from one language into another. Thus, or near this manner, was Horace his *Art of Poetry* translated by Ben Jonson. The second way is that of paraphrase, or translation with latitude, where the author is kept in view by the translator, so as never to be lost, and that too is admitted to be amplified, but not altered. Such is Mr. Waller's translation of Virgil's Fourth *Aeneid*. The third way is that of imitation, where the translator (if now he has not lost that name) assumes the liberty, not only to vary from the words and sense, but to forsake them both as he sees occasion; and taking only some general hints from the original, to run division on the groundwork, as he pleases. Such is Mr. Cowley's practice in turning two odes of Pindar, and one of Horace, into English.

Eighteenth-century audiences enjoyed comparing imitations with the original, not to check the "accuracy" of "translation," but rather to reap full enjoyment from the imitator's innovations on, and departures from, the classical text. Well aware of this appetite for comparison, booksellers (i.e., publishers) often printed the Latin along with the English. This kind of imitation was of course far removed from plagiarism, as Johnson pointed out in *Rambler* 143. In conclusion, it is fair to say that in the eighteenth century at least several men were indeed "great by imitation."

Some Directions in the Criticism of Poetry

The approaches used by eighteenth-century critics can be divided into six groups. One approach was to take a hard analytical look at the rules of art without actually doing away with them. This method is eloquently represented by the dialogues in Dryden's *Essay of Dramatic Poesy*, the ultimate effect of which is to take a stand not against rules per se but against foolish rules (e.g., the French rules for drama). A second approach was the effort to establish or examine parallels among the various arts, as in Dryden's *Parallel Betwixt Poetry and Painting*. The study of the "sister arts" was popular throughout the Augustan period. Another approach concentrated on the nature of the poet himself, as in Edward Young's *Conjectures on Original Composition*, which couches its arguments in a series of interesting paradoxes. For example, to be like the ancients is to be *unlike* them — that is, original and unprecedented. A fourth approach concentrated not on the poet but on the poem itself; Thomas Rymer's *Short View of Tragedy*, for example, lacerates Shakespeare's *Othello* for disobeying the rules. Still another group of critics studied the relations of art to the human psyche. The most important work in this "psychological" school was carried on by Addison in his series of *Spectators* on "The Pleasures of the Imagination" (nos. 411–21). In shifting the emphasis from the work itself to the individual's response to it, the influential Addison helped to pave the way for the subjectivism so popular in the second half of the eighteenth century. It would not be much of an exaggeration to say that in "The Pleasures of the Imagination" we are witnessing the birth of modern esthetics. The sixth and last group was somewhat more technical than the others, for it dealt with the nature of criticism itself; the major example here is of course Pope's *Essay on Criticism*.

The gradual changes in critical attitudes that took place from 1660 to 1800 are complex. However, one immediately notices a shift from emphasizing the general and the universal to stressing the particular and the unique; from a tendency to accept classical— or neoclassical—authority to an inclination to test precepts empirically; and from seeing the poet as a purveyor of "what oft was thought" to seeing him as an individual creative genius. What happens in the history of criticism from 1660 to 1800 (and this includes Wordsworth's *Preface to the Lyrical Ballads*) is not so much a matter of revolution as a matter of slow and steady development.

The Ancient-Modern Quarrel

One of the most colorful chapters in the history of criticism is the ancient-modern controversy that raged in England in the late seventeenth and early eighteenth centuries. Stated simply, the basic question was: Who were the best writers—the ancient Greeks and Romans or the modern Europeans? The first gauntlet was flung down by Sir William Temple, who published his *Essay Upon the Ancient and*

Modern Learning in 1690, vigorously siding with the ancients. He was attacked (primarily because of his slovenly scholarship rather than his opinion), and the battle was underway. Though no Augustan fits neatly into either category, a tentative division would be as follows: on the side of the ancients, Temple, Swift, Pope, Gay, Parnell, Congreve, and Rowe; on the moderns' side, Addison, Steele, Ambrose Philips, Tickell, Welsted, Dennis, and Gildon.

Some of the arguments used to support the ancients may be mentioned briefly. Nature, which poetry imitates, has steadily decayed since the Fall; because the early writers were chronologically closer to nature in its pristine state, they are the better writers. In addition, the ancients have stood the test of time; they have achieved immortality, which the moderns have yet to do. Moreover, English, because it is a structurally weak language, cannot endure—"And such as Chaucer is, shall Dryden be," as Pope said in his *Essay on Criticism*. But Latin and Greek had lasted for many centuries. Also, the Greeks and Romans frequently achieved the sublime, a feat seldom accomplished by modern writers. And the fact that the moderns usually imitated the ancients argued for the superiority of the ancients. Finally, it was obvious that the writings of the ancient world were vast storehouses of wisdom and morality.

However, there was more "evidence" on the side of the moderns. As even Temple had to admit, modern English writers had in fact produced a great deal of first-rate drama. And native English moderns could serve the patriotic causes of a country that was still not quite through with the process of establishing itself as a world power. Also, the ancients were frequently too lascivious or obscene in their writings—one had only to point to Juvenal the satirist. Further, the English language, rather than being structurally weak, was a wonderfully adaptable and flexible tongue, highly suited to the varieties of poetry. Such dynamic language, it could be argued, enabled English writers to achieve the sublime. On top of that, the modern writer, like a giant standing on a giant's shoulders, could see farther—he had ancient *plus* modern learning. As for the supposed decay of nature, that simply was not true. As Newton had shown, nature was fixed, unchanging: "One clear, unchanged, and universal light" *(Essay on Criticism)*. And the ancients are chronologically so far removed from the modern world that by and large they are irrelevant to it. Finally—and this was the most devastating of all—the moderns are *Christians* and the ancients are not.

Among the more important results of the quarrel were a partial breaking down of restraint and authority and a consequent growing emphasis on individualistic writing. On the other hand, there were many successful poetic reconciliations of ancient and modern materials, as in Pope's *Imitations of Horace* or Johnson's *London* and *The Vanity of Human Wishes,* both imitations of Juvenal.

The ancient-modern controversy of the turn of the seventeenth and eighteenth centuries was sharp and at times bitter. But the fact that it is readily observable should not allow us to forget that in a sense there is *always* an ancient-modern quarrel. Aristotle in his *Poetics* seems to look back on Homer with admiration but saves his greatest praise for Sophocles the "modern." The conflict continued among the classical Roman writers, to whom the Greeks were the "ancients." And in our own time, perhaps due to T. S. Eliot and the New Criticism, the Metaphysical poets of the earlier seventeenth century have often served as our "ancients," though not to everyone's satisfaction. The battle is never quite over, nor should it be.

Some Differences between the Augustans and the Romantics

What follows is a series of *general* distinctions between the Augustan and the Romantic modes. These are valid only as generalizations, and it is hoped that the reader will view them as introductory rather than as definitive. The information given below is merely a place for the newcomer to start the long and arduous task of working out his own final version of the complex relationships between the eighteenth century and the Romantic era.

One might well begin with attitudes toward nature, for that is what most generations of poets claim to follow or imitate. However, the "nature of nature" changes from age to age. That imitated by the Augustans was orderly, regular, and uniform, whereas that followed by the Romantics was irregular and sometimes wild and chaotic. Somewhat related to these views of nature is the neoclassical love of a stable social hierarchy, as opposed to the Romantic tendency toward revolution and away from the Great Chain of Being and the Golden Mean. And related to these political attitudes is the contrast between Augustan restraint and the Romantic eagerness to display emotion.

It is not surprising, then, that the Augustan tends to write in an impersonal manner, whereas the Romantic is much more personal or "lyrical." Whereas the Augustan accents the public and the general or universal, the Romantic emphasizes the private and the particular or unique. Perhaps that is why Romantic art is so often rather oblique, indirect, or even obscure, while the eighteenth century has a rage for clarity. The concern for clarity may explain the Augustan's love of broadly applicable abstractions, as opposed to the Romantic's love of the concrete but unexplained image or symbol. And it follows that the Romantic is much less didactic, working instead through suggestion and implication. The pursuit of clarity may also account for the tight and "logical" syntax of eighteenth-century poetry, which differs from the frequently loose or unconnected syntax of the early nineteenth century.

The Romantic unwillingness to be tethered by convention manifested itself in a rejection of most of the traditional Augustan genres, though in fact no poetry is totally ungeneric—even Wordsworth classified some of his works as "poems of fancy" or "poems of imagination."

The Romantics also rejected a major portion of the Roman antiquity so highly prized by the eighteenth century, but they replaced the Romans with the Greeks. It was, in a manner of speaking, a shift of antiquities, a transition from one neoclassicism to another. There may be a relationship between ancient Greek pantheism and the Romantic tendency to see God *in* nature, as opposed to the Augustan view that God is above, and separate from, the creation.

The scene in Romantic verse is often an isolated setting in rural nature, imbued with the presence of the divine spirit, whereas the eighteenth-century scene is most often in the town, bustling with the social affairs of men. It may have been the Augustan poet's interest in the broad canvas of the social scene that prevented him from writing narrative verse in any great quantity. On the other hand, Romantic poetry abounds with long passionate narratives of highly individualized heroes.

Thus the atmosphere of much early nineteenth-century writing is one of narrative flow, smoothly and freely associating from one thing to another; whereas the atmosphere of much Augustan work is one of increments, of concatenated arguments or epigrams. There may be a connection between the Romantic's propensity for narrative, which always involves transition and progression, and his essentially futuristic orientation, as opposed to the Augustan fascination with the actual and the immediate, the here and now. The dynamic futurism of the early nineteenth-century poet calls for a heavy use of verbs, the words of action and change; whereas the eighteenth-century writer leans heavily on adjectives, words that tend to stabilize experience by pinpointing the eternal qualities of things.

To the Romantic, however, the qualities of things are not eternal but *negotiable*. That the universe need not, or should not, be the way it is, is an attitude common in the poetry of the early nineteenth century. Romantic questioning of the cosmos ranges from mild dissatisfaction to Job-like defiance, which is at the opposite end of the scale from Pope's "whatever is, is right." Related to the Romantic poet's tendency to transfer the blame from man to the heavens is his belief that human nature is essentially good—so much so, that people actually have an innate ability to choose right over wrong, an ability seldom allowed to man by Augustan writers.

It follows, then, that although early nineteenth-century writers sometimes voice dissatisfaction with the universe, they also hold an essentially optimistic view. If things can change, why not for the better? The Augustan counterpart to this optimism was not so much pessimism as it was a kind of *staticism.* Things were not likely to change much, either for the better or the worse. It would not be far-fetched to associate this middle-of-the-road stance with the eighteenth-century accent on maturity or adulthood, which contrasts sharply with the Romantic emphasis on youth and the hopeful morning of existence. Thus children have a major and sympathetic part in Romantic poetry, whereas in Augustan verse they make very few appearances. When they do appear, they are often treated as though they were either inanimate objects or miniature adults.

The youthful idealism of Romanticism is Platonic in the sense that it tends to seek an ideal beyond the immediate surfaces of things. Romantics tend to see appearance as an outward and inferior manifestation of an inner ideal, a perfect ideal that man ought to pursue but will never completely grasp. Augustans, on the other hand, are Aristotelian in the sense that their ideals are the result of inferring or abstracting the general from the many particulars of reality.

The Transition from the Earlier
Seventeenth Century to the Augustan Age

The eighteenth century is in many ways an extension or continuation of the Renaissance. Thus the transition from the earlier seventeenth century to the Augustan Age is not as clear or well-defined as that from Augustan to Romantic. However, certain changes do stand out.

One notices immediately in the earlier seventeenth-century poets a tendency toward extravagant metaphors or far-fetched comparisons. Such extravagance was eschewed by the Augustans, who had a distrust of any discourse that strayed too far from the literal truth. In eighteenth-century poetry, the typical metaphor is one of modest brevity, its function being to illuminate the subject or prose sense of the poem, rather than to call strenuous attention to itself, as in the Metaphysical poets.

The Augustan's attitude toward metaphor is related to his view of wit, that part of the mind that sees similarities between things apparently unlike. The Augustans felt wit to be a necessary but rather wild and unstable faculty that was in constant need of check and restraint by judgment, which saw differences between things that were apparently *alike*.

One general difference between seventeenth and eighteenth-century poetry is that the former has about it an atmosphere of expansive all-inclusiveness, an implied thesis that all knowledge and experience can be placed under the same roof. Thus it is not uncommon to find yoked together in a metaphysical poem the large and the small, the foreign and the domestic, the strange and the familiar, the important and the trivial. Such juxtapositions offended the Augustans, whose verse strives for an atmosphere of proportion, of things discriminated from each other and put in their proper places, of sharp distinctions that are the work of judgment.

The eighteenth-century poet's distrust of figurative language also shows up in his scant use of classical mythology. The Renaissance writer, on the other hand, often gives the impression that he has room for every figure from Adonis to Zeus. The mythology of pre-Augustan verse is heavily indebted to Ovid's *Metamorphoses*, but just as important is his *Art of Love*, which helped to establish the rich love conventions of Shakespeare, Donne, and their contemporaries.

Here we may note another major difference between the two periods, for the eighteenth century produced relatively little love poetry. Such amorous effusions were foreign to an age that accented the public, the impersonal, and the non-lyrical. The Augustans admired Ovid's *Heroides* for their epistolary art and the heroic stature of the characters, but the *Metamorphoses* and the *Art of Love* had gone out of fashion.

The way that Renaissance and Augustan writers pick and choose among Ovid's several works illustrates the thesis that what happens in the change from one age to the next is not so much an abandoning of classical authority as a replacing of old precedents with new ones—even within one classical author! In a manner of speaking, there is no such thing as a period that is *not* neoclassical.

A large overriding distinction between the early

seventeenth century and the Augustan Age is that the earlier period often seems to be laboring under a burden of anxiety, gloom, and pessimism, which contrasts with the happier, if not optimistic, atmosphere of the eighteenth century. Under this general distinction a number of lesser distinctions can be subsumed. One is that the earlier seventeenth century makes frequent use of paradox, an expression of its anxiety, whereas the Augustans tend to replace or resolve paradox with balanced antithesis, as in their doctrine of the Golden Mean. To the Metaphysical poet, paradox is a permanent state; but in the eighteenth century, it is a transitional stage to pass through on the way to the ultimate harmony.

The early seventeenth-century poet's gloom and anxiety can also be seen in his concept of nature. Though he could allow for a higher kind of nature, a divinely ordered harmony, he often saw the earthbound nature of his immediate surroundings as corrupt and decadent, the result of Original Sin. He was inclined to believe that when Adam and Eve fell, terrestrial nature fell with them—how else could one explain the hideous jumble of the mountains, the awful wilderness of the forests, or the desolate waste of the sea?

Needless to say, the Augustans viewed nature through much rosier glasses. The mountains, forests, and oceans were lovely, even sublime, the result of God's handiwork. What had happened was that, between the two periods, the New Science, with Bacon in the forefront and Newton bringing up the rear, had chased the devil out of nature. The empiricism of the Augustans reduced considerably the level of superstition, though of course no age is entirely free of superstition. In any case, the Cliffs of Dover that were so ugly and frightening in *King Lear* became sublime in the eighteenth century.

The New Science was also partly responsible for the fact that Augustan poets were less concerned with religion. Although they were Christians like their seventeenth-century counterparts, they lived in an era when the church was no longer a dominant force in everyday life. Thus in the age of Dryden, Pope, and Johnson, it is unusual to find a major poet who like Donne, Herbert, or Crashaw devotes most or all of his career to religion. And when eighteenth-century poets do sing of God, they usually express security and harmony in their relationships with Him, not anxiety and strife as in the Metaphysical poets.

The anxiety, doubt, and pessimism of the earlier seventeenth century was related to the "New Philosophy." By the time of Donne, many intellectuals had come to believe the Copernican cosmology, which removed the earth from the center-of-the-universe position it had enjoyed under the old Ptolemaic system of concentric spheres. In the Copernican view, the sun no longer went around the earth, and man was no longer in the center of the Creation. The Augustans too were essentially Copernican in their view of the cosmos, but they felt no loss at being exiled to the sidelines of the universe; for as can be inferred from their doctrine of the Great Chain of Being, they believed that the center of the Creation was not a very desirable place to be. Also worth ponting out is that the Augustan cosmology was mechanistic rather than animistic as in the Renaissance. The eighteenth-century individual did not have to concern himself with the realms of magical spirits that had captured, baffled, and frightened the imagination of the earlier seventeenth century. However, if the clock-like Augustan cosmos was safer and quieter than that of the previous age, it was also less colorful. Such was the price of eliminating, chiefly through science, the spirits of evil that had flitted freely through the boisterous air of the Renaissance.

Bibliography

Chapter I

Familiar Epistle. Unfortunately modern scholarship has paid little attention to this important genre. The best piece of recent criticism is Jay A. Levine's "The Status of the Verse Epistle Before Pope," *SP*, LIX (1962). One way to study the Augustan familiar epistle writers is to study their great model, Horace. See Grant Showerman's *Horace and His Influence* (1922) and Caroline Goad's *Horace in the English Literature of the Eighteenth Century* (1918). See also Edward Fraenkel's *Horace* (1957) for a direct study of the ancient poet. An important eighteenth-century view is offered in *Spectator* 618.

Epigram and Epitaph. One of the best brief histories of the epigram-epitaph is Henry P. Dodd's introduction to his collection *The Epigrammatists* (1870); in spite of its age and its Victorian moralizing, it has seldom been bettered. An excellent recent critical study is *The Epigram in the English Renaissance* (1947) by H. H. Hudson; though it concentrates on the Renaissance, it can help to shed light on the Augustans. Less valuable is another modern study, G. R. Hamilton's *English Verse Epigram* (*Writers and Their Work*, no. 188, 1965), which tends to overquote and to offer more appreciation than criticism. More interesting reading is offered in R. W. Kelton-Cremer's "Lapidary Verse," *Proceedings of the British Academy*, XLV (1959). Some good general classical background is available in Paul Nixon's *Martial and Modern Epigram* (1927). Also useful is J. V. Cunningham's brief introduction to Pierre Nicole's *An Essay on the True and Apparent Beauty in which from Settled Principles is Rendered the Grounds for Choosing and Rejecting Epigrams* (*Augustan Reprint Society*, no. 24, Series IV, no. 5, 1950)—Nicole's essay itself is less useful. Other early writings on the epigram are: the introduction to Joshua Poole's *English Parnassus* (1657), fascinating for its almost comically catchall definition of "epigram"; the introduction (ascribed to William Oldys) to *A Collection of Epigrams* (1727), useful for its distinction between Martialian and *Greek Anthology* epigrams; and Samuel Johnson's *An Essay on Epitaphs* (Works), interesting for its attempt to furnish rules for writing epitaphs. It seems ironic that such a smallish genre as the epitaph-epigram has elicited such a volume of comment and criticism.

Fable. An excellent document that gives both modern and Augustan views is Robert Dodsley's *An Essay on the Fable* (1764), with an introduction by

Jeanne K. Welcher and Richard Dircks (*Augustan Reprint Society*, no. 112, 1965). See also Patricia M. Spacks's "John Gay: A Satirist's Progress," *Essays in Criticism*, XIV (1964), which deals with the several masks used by Gay; and Albert E. Graham's unpublished dissertation, "John Gay's Fables," *DA*, XXI, 2273 (1961), which has an introduction treating the fable as a genre. In addition to Dodsley, mentioned above, see two other Augustans: Addison, *Spectators* 183 and 512; and Johnson, *Life of Gay* (Works).

Mock-Heroic, Burlesque, and the Minor Mock-Genres. A useful, if somewhat dilettantish, study is George Kitchin's *A Survey of Burlesque and Parody in English* (1931); more scholarly is R. P. Bond's definitive study, *English Burlesque Poetry, 1700–1750* (1932), which offers some sharp defining of terms, a summary of eighteenth-century criticism of burlesque or mock-heroic, and a register of mock or burlesque pieces. Also useful is a much earlier work, W. M. Dixon's *English Epic and Heroic Poetry* (1912), especially for *Hudibras* and *The Rape of the Lock.* First-rate criticism is offered by Ian Jack's *Augustan Satire* (1952), which stresses that a mock-heroic piece may actually have a number of levels of style and several different targets. On the Hudibrastic influence, see Edward A. Richards's *Hudibras in the Burlesque Tradition* (1937), which includes a register of "Hudibrastic" poems.

Formal Verse Satire. The best general treatment of this tradition is John Heath-Stubbs's *The Verse Satire* (1969). It covers material from ancient to

modern times, offers many quotations, and is very
brief and readable. On the "A-B" structure, see Mary
Claire Randolph's "The Structural Design of Formal
Verse Satire," *PQ*, XXI (1942). Ian Jack's first-rate
Augustan Satire (1952) may be slightly flawed by
Jack's asserting that formal verse satire is scarce in
the eighteenth century and then proceeding to dis-
cuss it at length and with great intelligence. The
most interesting Augustan document is Dryden's
*Discourse Concerning the Original and Progress of
Satire* (1693).

Prologue-Epilogue. The definitive study of this
genre in the 1700s is Mary E. Knapp's *Prologues and
Epilogues of the Eighteenth Century* (1961), though it
has little to say about style and tends to give Romanticism too much credit for speeding the demise of the
prologue-epilogue. Mark Van Doren's *John Dryden:
A Study of His Poetry* (1920; rev., 1946) studies
Dryden's prologues and epilogues in detail, making
many observations that could apply to other writers
in the genre. A worthwhile Augustan document is
Spectator 341, which stresses the separability of the
prologue-epilogue and the play.

Chapter II

Pastoral. Always essential to discussions of pastoral
is William Empson's *Some Versions of Pastoral* (1938),
which develops the idea that pastoral "puts the complex into the simple." For some general background
of pastoral, see E. K. Chambers's introduction to
English Pastorals (n.d.); Chambers is also a good example of the bias of modern readers against

Augustan pastoral verse. For the survey of the many forms that pastoral could take in the period, see R. F. Jones's "Eclogue Types in English Poetry of the Eighteenth Century," *JEGP*, XXIX (1930). Also useful is Marion K. Bragg's "The Formal Eclogue in Eighteenth-Century England," *University of Maine Studies*, ser. 2, no. 6 (1926). A great deal of information on the eighteenth-century traditions of pastoral, and the critical arguments surrounding them, may be found in J. E. Congleton's *Theories of Pastoral Poetry in England, 1684–1798* (1952), marred slightly by Congleton's overestimation of the Romantic writers of pastoral. Another useful study is Lee Andrew Elioseff's "Pastorals, Politics and the Idea of Nature in the Reign of Queen Anne," *Journal of Aesthetics and Art Criticism*, XXI (1963). A very good basic guide that treats classical as well as neoclassical material is John Heath-Stubbs's *The Pastoral* (1969). Famous and useful Augustan documents are Pope's *Discourse on Pastoral Poetry* and Johnson's harsh attack on Milton's *Lycidas* in his *Life of Milton*. See also Johnson's *Ramblers* 36 and 37.

Georgic. The definitive work on the georgic is Dwight L. Durling's *Georgic Tradition in English Poetry* (1935), though one could wish for more actual criticism and less discussion of form and content. Another useful work, though much less sophisticated, is Marie L. Lilly's *The Georgic* (1919). A recent work that can be called "critical" in the true sense of the term is John Chalker's *The English Georgic: A Study in the Development of a Form* (1969), though Chalker slights the sociological implications of the genre. Two older but still useful treatments of the

Virgilian influence are Wilfred P. Mustard's "Virgil's *Georgics* and the British Poets," *American Journal of Philology*, XXIX (1908) and Elizabeth Nitchie's *Vergil and the English Poets* (1919). No student of the georgic will want to overlook Addison's important *Essay on Vergil's Georgics* (*Works*).

Topographical Poem. Regarding subject matter, the definitive book on the topographical poem is R. A. Aubin's *Topographical Poetry in Eighteenth-Century England* (1936), though one could wish that Aubin had expanded his definition of the topographical poem beyond pieces that deal merely with "specifically named actual localities." Aubin includes a large register of topographical verse. Also useful is Chapter VII, "A Note on Local Verse," in Dwight L. Durling's *Georgic Tradition in English Poetry* (1935). See also R. D. Havens's *The Influence of Milton on English Poetry* (1922), p. 249 *ff.* For elaborate readings of *Cooper's Hill* and *Windsor Forest*, see Earl R. Wasserman's *The Subtler Language* (1959). A recent challenge to Aubin's time-honored position as dean of the topographical critics is John Wilson Foster's "A Redefinition of Topographical Poetry," *JEGP*, LXIX (1970). The best Augustan statement on topographical poetry occurs in Johnson's *Life of Denham*.

Reflective-Descriptive Tradition. Although the works of Dwight L. Durling and R. A. Aubin, cited above under the Topographical Poem, are tangentially useful, the best piece of criticism centered directly on the tradition is Norman Callan's "Augustan Reflective Poetry," in *From Dryden to*

Johnson, ed. Boris Ford (1957). For a view of the way in which a reflective-descriptive poet could assemble vast and various materials, see A. D. McKillop's *The Background of Thomson's Seasons* (1942). For the contention that Thomson thought "art" was "knowledge," see Ralph Cohen's "An Introduction to *The Seasons,*" *Southern Review,* III (1968). In the eighteenth century, Johnson's *Life of Thomson* is useful.

"Graveyard School." Two reputable twentieth-century works are Amy L. Reed's *The Background of Gray's Elegy* (1924) and John W. Draper's *The Funeral Elegy and the Rise of English Romanticism* (1929), though both deal more with melancholy than with specific graveyard poetry. More pertinent are some remarks on the "night-piece" in Chapter IX of James Sutherland's *Preface to Eighteenth-Century Poetry* (1948). For a discussion of the widely held belief that Milton's minor poems were influential in the melancholy and graveyard traditions, see R. D. Havens's "Literature of Melancholy," *MLN,* XXIV (1909).

Poetic Diction. Probably the best treatment of poetic diction in relation to individual words is Geoffrey Tillotson's pair of essays, "Augustan Poetic Diction: I" and "Augustan Poetic Diction: II," both collected in his *Augustan Studies* (1961). John Arthos's *The Language of Natural Description in Eighteenth Century Poetry* (1949) intelligently investigates poetic diction in its relation to science. More recent views are in William Powell Jones's *The Rhetoric of Science* (1966). An older but still useful general study is Thomas Quayle's *Poetic Diction*

(1924), interesting for its efforts to overthrow the biases against the Augustans that were still strong in the 1920s. C. V. Deane's *Aspects of Eighteenth-Century Nature Poetry* (1935) is incisive, especially on periphrasis. Another incisive treatment is Chapter XVI, "Poetic Diction: Wordsworth and Coleridge," of Cleanth Brooks and William K. Wimsatt's *Literary Criticism: A Short History* (1957). On the device of personification, three items are especially useful. First, Bertrand Bronson's "Personification Reconsidered," in his *Facets of the Enlightenment* (1968), sees tensions in the way personifications reconcile abstract-concrete and general-particular. Second, Earl R. Wasserman's "The Inherent Values of Eighteenth-Century Personification," *PMLA*, LXV (1950), discusses the way in which personification is "based upon the divinely arranged analogy of the physical and moral worlds." Third, Chester F. Chapin's *Personification in Eighteenth-Century Poetry* (1955) attempts to make a distinction between "allegorical" and "metaphorical" personifications. For some insights into the various levels of poetic diction, see Donald Davie's *Purity of Diction in English Verse* (1952). For some comments on the use of the article *the* in Augustan verse, see Ian Jack's *Augustan Satire* (1952), particularly the chapter on "The Vanity of Human Wishes." An ironic but revealing eighteenth-century document is Pope's *Peri Bathous: Of the Art of Sinking in Poetry* (*Works*).

Chapter III

Ode. A useful history of this genre is George Shuster's *The English Ode from Milton to Keats*

(1940), which continues Robert Shafer's *The English Ode to 1660* (1918). Nearly as important as Shuster is Chapter IX of James Sutherland's *Preface to Eighteenth-Century Poetry* (1948), containing less history and more criticism than Shuster's work. For some interesting distinctions between "sublime" and "beautiful" as they relate to the ode, see Norman Maclean's "From Action to Image," in *Critics and Criticism*, ed. R. S. Crane (1952). Although her study stops at Cowley, Carol Madison's *Apollo and the Nine: A History of the Ode* (1960) contains some valuable background. Very brief and clear is John Heath-Stubbs's *The Ode* (1969). Two important Augustan essays are: William Congreve's *Discourse on the Pindaric Ode*, prefixed to his *A Pindaric Ode Humbly Offered to the Queen* (1706); and Edward Young's *On Lyric Poetry*, prefixed to his *Ocean: An Ode* (1728). See also Abraham Cowley's *Ode on Liberty*, which describes what was then thought to be the "Pindaric Way."

Song. For an effort to group songs by subject matter, see Catherine Walsh Peltz's "The Neo-Classical Lyric," *ELH*, XI (1944); and several works by Oswald Doughty: *English Lyric in the Age of Reason* (1922), *Forgotten Lyrics of the Eighteenth Century* (1924), and "Eighteenth-Century Song," *ES*, VII (1925). Anyone who writes on the Augustan song will be indebted to Peltz and Doughty, but it is regrettable that their work appeared early enough to succumb to the now-outmoded view that the Augustans worshipped reason to the almost total exclusion of heart and imagination. A more recent study, which goes a little deeper, is Norman Maclean's "From Action to Image," in *Critics and Criticism*, ed. R. S. Crane (1952). Interesting eighteenth-century views appear in John Aikin's *Essays on Song-Writing* (1774) and in Ambrose Philips's letter on song-writing in *The Guardian*, no. 16.

Hymn. The best brief survey of the eighteenth-century hymn is George Sampson's "The Century of Divine Songs," a lively and readable article in *Proceedings of the British Academy*, XXIX (1943). Also useful as brief guides are Louise M. North's *The Psalms and Hymns of Protestantism* (1936); Arthur Pollard's *English Hymns* (*Writers and Their Work*, no. 123, 1960); and Ralph Lawrence's "The English Hymn," *Essays and Studies*, new ser., VII (1954). Donald Davie's *Purity of Diction in English Verse* (1952) has an incisive literary-critical chapter on "The Classicism of Charles Wesley." Book-length treatments of the hymn are Henry Bett's *The Hymns of Methodism and Their Literary Relations* (1913) and Louis F. Benson's *The English Hymn: Its Development and Use in Worship* (1962). A revealing Augustan document is Isaac Watt's *Preface* to his *Horae Lyricae* (1706). See also Johnson's *Life of Watts (Lives of the Poets)*, in which Johnson doubts that it is possible to write first-rate religious poetry.

Sonnet. The best treatment and survey of the sonnet in the eighteenth century appears in Chapter XIX of R. D. Havens's *The Influence of Milton on English Poetry* (1922), from which much of the information in my notes on the sonnet is taken. Some years ago, *MLN* published a number of pieces on the eighteenth-century sonnet. Some of these are: Clarissa Rinaker's "Thomas Edwards and the Sonnet

Revival," XXXIV (1919); Allan D. McKillop's "Some Details of the Sonnet Revival," XXXIX (1924); R. P. McCutcheon's "Notes on the Occurrence of the Sonnet and Blank Verse," XL (1925); and R. A. Aubin's "Some Eighteenth-Century Sonnets," XLIX (1934)— all of these writings contain short criticisms as well as textual information.

Ballad. The writings about the ballad are voluminous, and this bibliographical note mentions only a few of the outstanding ones. Two essential books for the study of eighteenth-century balladry are Sigurd Hustvedt's *Ballad Criticism in Scandinavia and Great Britain During the Eighteenth Century* (1916) and Albert B. Friedman's *The Ballad Revival* (1961). An interesting article is Keith Stewart's "The Ballad and the Genres in the Eighteenth Century," *ELH*, XXIV (1957), which argues that the ballad was instrumental in breaking down the traditional genres of Augustan poetry. For musical implications, see Claude M. Simpson's *The British Broadside Ballad and Its Music* (1966). A recent comprehensive treatment of the ballad in general is David C. Fowler's *A Literary History of the Popular Ballad* (1968). An informative eighteenth-century document is John Aikin's *Essay on Ballads and Pastoral Songs*, which appears with his *Essays on Song-Writing* (1774). Also important are *Spectators* 70 and 74, in which Addison writes in detail on the famous ballad *Chevy Chase*. Needless to say, the introductory matter in Percy's *Reliques* (1765) is valuable.

Anacreontic. Since this is a very minor genre, it is reasonable—though disappointing—to expect that it has received little attention from modern scholars.

Even today, Francis Fawkes, the eighteenth-century translator of Anacreon, is a very good source. See his introduction and notes to his *The Works of Anacreon* (1760). Some useful information about Anacreon and his tradition can be found in the introduction to volume II of J. M. Edmund's *Elegy and Iambus* (1931). A popularistic but worthwhile essay is Thomas Moore's *Remarks on Anacreon*, prefixed to his translation of Anacreon (1800).

Elegy. Though somewhat dated now and too "sociological" in its approach, John W. Draper's *Funeral Elegy and the Rise of English Romanticism* (1929) is still helpful. There are several very useful Augustan documents: Joseph Trapp's "Lecture XIII: Of Elegy," in his *Lectures on Poetry* (1742); William Shenstone's *Prefatory Essay on Elegy* (1725?), prefixed to his twenty-six *Elegies*; and Johnson's *Life of Milton* *(Lives of the Poets)*, containing the famous attack on *Lycidas.*

Chapter IV

Epic. A still useful early twentieth-century work is W. M. Dixon's *English Epic and Heroic Poetry* (1912). On the critical tradition, see H. T. Swedenberg's excellent *Theory of the Epic in England, 1650–1800* (1944). The best recent study of the English epic is E. M. W. Tillyard's *English Epic and its Background* (1954). A short but valuable discussion is the section on "Heroic Verse" in Douglas Bush's *English Literature in the Earlier Seventeenth Century* (1945). Of the mass of epic criticism produced by the Augustans, two of the most revealing are Davenant's *Preface to Gondibert*, with the answer by Thomas

Hobbes (1650), and Samuel Wesley's *Essay on Heroic Poetry* (1697). Interesting for simultaneously fighting and succumbing to neoclassical prejudices are Addison's *Spectators* on *Paradise Lost* (nos. 267, 273, 279, 285, 291, 297, 303, 309, 315, and 321).

Heroic Epistle. Recent criticism has paid little attention to this genre. See H. Dörrie's "L'Épître Héroïque dans les Littératures Modernes . . . Epistulae Herodium d'Ovide," *RLC*, XL (1966). See also Robert K. Root's *Poetical Career of Alexander Pope* (1938), p. 96 *ff.* Sometimes introductions to editions of Ovid can yield valuable information, as in Evelyn S. Shuckburgh's edition, *P. Ovidii Nasonis: Heroidium Epistulae* (1896). An excellent piece of Augustan criticism occurs in Section VI of Joseph Warton's *Essay on the Genius and Writings of Pope* (1756 and 1782). And in the Renaissance there is Drayton's interesting introduction to his *England's Heroicall Epistles* (1619).

Medieval or Gothic Tradition. Unfortunately, Gothic prose has received far more attention than the poetry of this tradition. However, some good information can be found in W. J. Courthope's *History of English Poetry* (1905), vol. V, Chapter XII. For some excellent cultural—as well as literary—background, see Kenneth Clark's *The Gothic Revival* (1929). For a very scholarly treatment of the historical background, see Samuel Kliger's *The Goths in England* (1952). For attitudes of Augustan scholars toward the medieval material, see Arthur Johnston's *Enchanted Ground: The Study of Medieval Romance in the Eighteenth Century* (1964). A good treatment of the kind of fright-peddling that occurs in much late-eighteenth-century verse is Patricia Meyer Spack's *The Insistence of Horror: Aspects of the Supernatural in Late-Eighteenth-Century Poetry* (1962). There are many writings on the term "Gothic." Some of the better ones are: A. E. Longueil's "The Word 'Gothic' in Eighteenth-Century Criticism," *MLN*, XXXVIII (1923); William C. Holbrook's "The Adjective *Gothique* in the Eighteenth Century," *MLN*, LVI (1941); and a good part of Kliger, mentioned above. For the relationship between Gothicism and nature, see A. O. Lovejoy's "The First Gothic Revival and the Return to Nature," in his *Essays in the History of Ideas* (1948). An interesting Augustan document on the Gothic is Bishop Richard Hurd's *Letters on Chivalry and Romance* (1762), which vigorously defends the medieval mode.

Oriental Tradition. Though concentrated on prose and written many years ago, Martha Conant's *The Oriental Tale in England in the Eighteenth Century* (1908) is still an excellent study; its divisions of Oriental tales into imaginative, philosophical, moral, and satirical are categories that frequently apply to the verse as well as the prose. A study devoted to the verse is Edna Osborne's *Oriental Diction and Theme in English Verse, 1740–1840*, in *Bulletin of the University of Kansas: Humanistic Studies*, II (1916). For some more literary background, see John D. Yohannan's "The Persian Poetry Fad in England, 1770–1825," *Comparative Literature*, IV (1952). Perhaps the best treatment of the cultural background—"Sharawadgi," interior decorating, and the like—is A. O. Lovejoy's "The Chinese Origin of Romanticism," in his *Essays in the History of Ideas* (1948). A lengthier study is William W. Appleton's *A Cycle of Cathay: The Chinese Vogue in England During the Seventeenth and Eighteenth Centuries* (1951). Interesting contemporary documents are Sir William Temple's *Essay Upon Heroick Virtue* (1701) and William Collins's brief preface to his *Persian Eclogues* (1742).

The Sublime. Scholars generally agree that the definitive book on the sublime is Samuel H. Monk's *The Sublime* (1960). Another very useful study is Walter J. Hipple, Jr.'s *The Beautiful, The Sublime, and the Picturesque in Eighteenth-Century British Aesthetic Theory* (1957). For some counter-statements, see R. S. Crane's review of Monk's book in *PQ*, XV (1936), which argues that the sublime, rather than helping to usher in Romanticism, merely furnished new rules. See also Marjorie H. Nicholson's *Mountain Gloom and Mountain Glory: The Development of the Aesthetics of the Infinite* (1959); she feels that the sublime was a doctrine in England long before Longinus was popular, reasoning that the New Science of the mid-seventeenth century helped to make nature attractive and to prepare the way for transport and astonishment at nature's triumphs. By far the most rewarding eighteenth-century document is Edmund Burke's *A Philosophical Enquiry into the Origin of Our Ideas of the Sublime and Beautiful* (1752). Needless to say, the fountainhead is Longinus himself, *On the Sublime.*

Sensibility. The best readable work on this topic is Louis I. Bredvold's *The Natural History of Sensibility* (1962). Also interesting is Northrop Frye's "Towards Defining an Age of Sensibility," in *Eighteenth-Cen-*

tury English Literature, ed. James L. Clifford (1959). Frye distinguishes poem as "product" (writing that gives an impression of finish and finality) from poem as "process" (writing that seems, although completed, to be in the process of composition, as though the writer is uncertain about what is coming next); sensibility, Frye says, is "process." This uncertainty of intent was touched on in an earlier essay, Bertrand Bronson's "The Pre-Romantic or Post-Augustan Mode," *ELH,* XX (1953), which sheds a great deal of light on sensibility. Still valid is R. S. Crane's "Suggestions Towards a Genealogy of the 'Man of Feeling,'" *ELH,* I (1934), collected in his *The Idea of the Humanities* (1967). Like Bredvold, Crane sees the origins of sensibility in the seventeenth century.

Chapter V

The opening pages of this chapter are in themselves a kind of bibliography, commenting critically on a number of works. Therefore in this section there is little left to do other than name those already discussed and add a few things to the list. This chapter has touched on the following items in the order in which they are mentioned here:

Northrop Frye, *Anatomy of Criticism* (1957)

Maynard Mack, "The Muse of Satire," *Yale Review,* XLI (1951)

Philip Pinkus, "Satire and Saint George," *Queen's Quarterly,* Spring (1963)

Alvin Kernan, *The Cankered Muse* (1959)

Edward W. Rosenheim, Jr., *Swift and the Satirist's Art* (1963)

T. S. Eliot, *Poetry in the Eighteenth Century*
(1930); originally appeared as an introduction to Johnson's imitations of Juvenal; in
Boris Ford, ed., *From Dryden to Johnson*
(1957)

Ian Jack, *Augustan Satire* (1952)

Robert C. Elliott, *The Power of Satire* (1960)

James Sutherland, *English Satire* (1958)

Sigmund Freud, *Jokes and Their Relation to the
Unconscious* (transl. 1960)

Henri Bergson, *Laughter* (1900)

Basil Willey, *The Eighteenth-Century Background* (1940)

The most illuminating Augustan treatise on the
subject is Dryden's *Discourse Concerning the Original and Progress of Satire*. The present writer has also
succumbed to the temptation to write about satire:
see Peter Thorpe, "Great Satire and the Fragmented
Norm," *Satire Newsletter*, Spring (1967); "The Eco-
nomics of Satire," *Western Humanities Review*, Summer (1969); "Thinking in Octagons: Further Reflections on Norms in Satire," *Satire Newsletter*, Spring
(1970); "Necessity, Free Will, and Satire," *Satire
Newsletter*, Spring (1971); and "Satire as Pre-Com-
edy," *Genre*, Spring (1971). Several other recent
works on satire are worth mentioning: Gilbert
Highet, *The Anatomy of Satire* (1962), very good on
the classical tradition; Ronald Paulson, *The Fictions of
Satire* (1967), a technical study of satire's imagery;
and Matthew Hodgart, *Satire* (1969), a light and
readable general survey. On the rise and fall of verse
satire in the eighteenth century, see two pieces by
Andrew M. Wilkinson, "The Rise of English Verse

Satire in the Eighteenth Century," *ES*, XXXIV (1953);
and "The Decline of English Verse Satire in the Middle Years of the Eighteenth Century," *RES*, ser. 2, III
(1952). The latter article, in arguing that sentiment
caused the death of satire, overlooks the possibility
that sentiment could *cause* satire.

The amount of useful criticism on satire is
bewildering. For the newcomer, one way out of the
bewilderment is to read three first-rate books on the
topic and temporarily forget about the rest. Ian
Jack's *Augustan Satire* (1952) is by far the best book
on verse satire in the eighteenth century. The two
best general treatments of satire are Northrop Frye's
Anatomy of Criticism (1957) and Alvin Kernan's *The
Cankered Muse* (1959).

Chapter VI

Heroic Couplet. The best short treatment of the
heroic couplet's relationship to the Golden Mean is
George Williamson's "The Rhetorical Pattern of
Neoclassical Wit," *MP*, XXXIII (1935), reprinted in his
Seventeenth-Century Contexts (1960). The best comprehensive treatment of the couplet is William Bow-
man Piper's *The Heroic Couplet* (1969), which furnishes a thorough history spanning two centuries;
Piper illustrates his points with generous quotations. A good book on the late Augustan couplet is
Wallace Cable Brown's *The Triumph of Form: A Study
of the Later Masters of the Heroic Couplet* (1948),
which centers on Gay, Johnson, Churchill, Young,
Cowper, Goldsmith, and Crabbe. For the early history of the couplet see (in addition to Piper) Ruth
Wallterstein's "The Development of the Rhetoric and

Meter of the Heroic Couplet, Especially in 1625–1645," *PMLA*, L (1935). For the post-Popean couplet, see Earl R. Wasserman's "The Return of the Enjambed Couplet," *ELH*, VII (1940). On the syntax in the couplet, consult Donald Davie's *Articulate Energy* (1954). For a version of the old argument that Ben Jonson was a crucial influence in the development of the couplet, see Felix Schelling's 1898 *PMLA* article, "Ben Jonson and the Classical School," reprinted in *Essential Articles: English Augustan Backgrounds,* ed. Bernard N. Schilling (1961). John A. Jones's study, *Pope's Couplet Art* (1969), though focused on Pope, is useful in a study of the couplet in general. Occasionally, couplet writers, after the manner of Dryden, insert a triplet into their verse; for a study of this mannerism, see Conrad A. Balliet's "The History and Rhetoric of the Triplet," *PMLA*, LXXX (1965). The most revealing eighteenth-century document on the heroic couplet is Edward Bysshe's *Art of English Poetry* (1702).

Blank Verse. Highly informative reading on blank verse in the period is provided by R. D. Havens's *The Influence of Milton on English Poetry* (1922), which contains, among other things, some useful statistics on the occurrence of blank verse in the Augustan Age. Also helpful is Chapter V of Enid Hamer's basic but useful *The Metres of English Poetry* (1930). See also a short article by R. P. McCutcheon, "Notes on the Occurrence of the Sonnet and Blank Verse," *MLN*, XL (1925).

Elegiac or Heroic Stanza. The best source of information about the elegiac or heroic stanza is George

Saintsbury's *History of English Prosody* (1908), vol. II, Book VII, Chapter I. See also Chapter VIII of Enid Hamer's well-written *The Metres of English Poetry* (1930). For Augustan statements, see William Davenant's *Preface to Gondibert* (published with a response from Hobbes, 1650) and William Shenstone's *A Prefatory Essay on Elegy* (written 1725?), usually appended to his twenty-six *Elegies*.

The Four-Stress Couplet and Hudibrastics. Centered on the Renaissance but partially relevant to the eighteenth century is Elbert N. S. Thompson's "The Octosyllabic Couplet," *PQ*, XVIII (1939). Also useful is Enid Hamer's *The Metres of English Poetry* (1930), Chapter II. An account of the "proper" placing of accents in the octosyllabic couplet can be found in Chapter I, Section II of Edward Bysshe's *Art of English Poetry* (1702).

Spenserian Stanza. Two very thorough pieces of work were done long ago but are still extremely useful; these are two articles by E. P. Morton: "The Spenserian Stanza before 1700," *MP*, IV (1907); and "The Spenserian Stanza in the Eighteenth Century," *MP*, X (1913). See also J. N. Hook's "Three Imitations of Spenser," *MLN*, LV (1940). Also useful is Earl R. Wasserman's *Elizabethan Poetry in the Eighteenth Century* (1947). Some interesting Augustan sentiments about Spenser appear in *Spectator* 540, by Steele. For a defense of allegory and an attack on Spenser's diction and stanza form, see Samuel Johnson's *Rambler* 121 (see also his *Lives of the Poets: West; Shenstone;* and *Thomson*).

Chapter VII

The Great Chain of Being. The definitive work on this idea is A. O. Lovejoy's famous *The Great Chain of Being* (1936). Interesting Augustan documents are *Spectator* 519 and the First Epistle of Pope's *Essay on Man*. For an attempt to establish a relationship between the Chain of Being and the political structure, see Soame Jenyns's *A Free Enquiry into the Nature and Origin of Evil* (1757), vigorously attacked by Johnson in the *Literary Magazine* (1757) in 3 consecutive issues, nos. 13, 14, 15.

The Golden Mean. Perhaps because of the neatness and simplicity of this concept, modern scholarship has paid little attention to it. A good study of the relationship between the Golden Mean and the structure of the heroic couplet is George Williamson's "The Rhetorical Pattern of Neoclassical Wit," *MP*, XXXIII (1935), reprinted in his *Seventeenth-Century Contexts* (1960). One approach is to go directly to the fountainhead, Aristotle's *Nichomachean Ethics*, 2.9, in which the Golden Mean is formulated in great detail but with great clarity. See also the use of the idea in Horace's Second Epistle of the First Book. In the eighteenth century, the most sustained and eloquent expression of the Golden Mean is John Pomfret's *The Choice* (1700), of which Johnson said, "Perhaps no composition in our language has been oftener perused."

Reason. Two earlier twentieth-century works are still very useful: Alfred W. Benn's *A History of English Rationalism*, 2 vols. (1906) and Oliver Elton's

"Reason and Enthusiasm in the Eighteenth Century," *Essays and Studies*, X (1924). See also Henry Pettit's, "The Limits of Reason as Literary Theme in the English Enlightenment," in *Studies on Voltaire and the Eighteenth Century*, ed. Theodore Besterman, 1963, vol. XXVI. In the Augustan period, for sheer devastation, there is nothing finer than Rochester's *Satire Against Mankind* (1675). Equally devastating but much more elaborate in its thought is Hume's *Treatise of Human Nature* (1739–1740).

Rules. Useful in investigating the rules is J. W. H. Atkins's basic *English Literary Criticism, Seventeenth and Eighteenth Centuries* (1951), especially the first three chapters. See also William K. Wimsatt and Cleanth Brooks's *Literary Criticism: A Short History* (1957), especially Chapters X, XI, and XII. The most interesting contemporary document for looking at the rules from several angles is Dryden's *Essay of Dramatic Poesy* (1668).

Imitation. There are several useful recent works on eighteenth-century imitation. On a scale moving from the clearest and the most readable to the most difficult, we note: the chapter on "The Rationale of Imitation" in *The Poetics of Reason* (1968) by Emerson Marks; *The Formal Strain* (1969) by Howard D. Weinbrot; and "Imitation as Freedom," by William K. Wimsatt, in *New Literary History*, I (1970). Revealing Augustan writings are Dryden's *Preface Concerning Ovid's Epistles* (1863) and Johnson's *Rambler* 143.

Some Directions in the Criticism of Poetry. The most useful item here, and the source for my note on this topic, is R. S. Crane's "English Neoclassical Criticism: An Outline-Sketch," in *Critics and Criticism*, ed. R. S. Crane (1952). Also useful are Chapters X through XV of William K. Wimsatt and Cleanth Brooks's *Literary Criticism: A Short History* (1957). For a more basic approach, see J. W. H. Atkins's *English Literary Criticism, Seventeenth and Eighteenth Centuries* (1951), passim. A very good sketch of directions in later eighteenth-century criticism can be found in George Sherburn's *The Restoration and the Eighteenth Century* (1967), Part III, Chapter II. The best collection of Augustan critical essays is *Eighteenth-Century Critical Essays*, ed. Scott Elledge, 2 vols. (1961). For critics before 1700, see *Critical Essays of the Seventeenth Century*, ed. J. E. Spingarn, 3 vols. (1908–1909).

The Ancient-Modern Quarrel. The definitive work on this event is R. F. Jones's *Ancients and Moderns* (1936; reissued, 1961). See also H. Rigault's *Histoire de la Querelle des Anciens et Modernes* (1956). Since much of the quarrel centered on the pastoral, it is instructive to read J. E. Congleton's *Theories of Pastoral Poetry in England, 1684–1798* (1952). If one wishes to mix his instruction with pleasure, there are few writings on the ancient-modern quarrel more appropriate than Swift's *Battle of the Books* (1704).

Some Differences between the Augustans and the Romantics. A great deal has been written on this vast topic. Five very good books are mentioned here. The earliest is Oliver Elton's *Survey of English Literature, 1780–1830*, 2 vols. (1912), which gives a readable and orthodox view. A famous work of scholarship is Ernest Bernbaum's *Guide Through the Romantic Movement* (1943), focused chiefly on the Romantic side. Part of the well-known *Oxford History of English Literature* is W. L. Renwick's *English Literature, 1789-1815* (1963). For a greater amount of criticism in proportion to literary history, see M. H. Abrams's *The Mirror and the Lamp* (1953). Probably the best one to begin with—because of its brevity, liveliness, and clarity—is Walter Jackson Bate's *From Classic to Romantic* (1946).

The Transition from the Earlier Seventeenth Century to the Augustan Age. Four very useful works are: George Williamson's *The Donne Tradition* (1930); R. L. Sharp's *From Donne to Dryden* (1940); G. Walton's *Metaphysical to Augustan* (1955); and Basil Willey's *The Seventeenth-Century Background* (1934). The last-named, which deals more with intellectual background than with literature, is the most interesting. The other three are more directly focused on the literary scene.

Index